CROSS VIEWS

Story Dramas
That Teach the Faith

Dean Nadasdy

CPH
SAINT LOUIS

To the staff and members of Cross View Lutheran Church, Edina, Minnesota, who first presented many of these dramas. They know the power of the fire, the ashes, and the resurrection.

All Scripture quotations are taken from the HOLY BIBLE, NEW INTERNATIONAL VERSION®. NIV®. Copyright © 1973, 1978, 1984 by International Bible Society. Used by permission of Zondervan Publishing House. All rights reserved.

Copyright © 1996 Concordia Publishing House
3558 S. Jefferson Avenue, St. Louis, MO 63118-3968
Manufactured in the United States of America

Library of Congress Cataloging-in-Publication Data

Nadasdy, Dean, 1947-

    Cross views : story dramas that teach the faith / Dean Nadasdy.
      p. cm.
    Includes index.
    ISBN 0-570-04864-8
    1. Drama in public worship. 2. Drama in Christian education. 3. Christian drama, American.
    4. Lutheran Church–Missouri Synod–Doctrines. 5. Lutheran Church–Doctrines. I. Title.
    BV289.N33 1996
    246<.7–dc20
                                              96-10675

                                                      CIP

1   2   3   4   5   6   7   8   9   10   05   04   03   02   01   00   99   98   97   96

Contents

Repentance and Renewal

Hope, fellowship, and praise come to those who rise from the ashes.

In subtle, even modest ways, we deny our Lord; yet we find forgiveness for our denials in Jesus Christ.

The Pharisee and tax collector struggle within each of us.

Christ is coming. Are we ready?

All people, no matter how pious, come under the scrutiny of God's Law.

We have many options when it comes to coping with guilt. Christians overcome guilt by trusting in Christ.

Christ's death counts as ours. Faith makes us one with Christ in death.

Faith

To have God on our side brings great assurance. But are we just as sure that we are on God's side?

We may point our finger at God and accuse, but through it all, God loves us and asks for continued trust.

God asks for an appointment.

Hope

Witness and Servanthood

Witness and Service

Introduction

Drama Belongs in the Church

For pure drama, nothing surpasses the dynamic of the Christian faith. For the Christian and for the church, Christianity is as dramatic as a resurrection from ashes. If drama is about life and death, Christianity is about daily life and death, daily ashes and daily resurrection.

If drama is about conflict, the Christian faith brings the tensions of Law/Gospel, judgment/grace, saint/sinner, now/not yet, and the list goes on.

If drama is about character development, the Holy Spirit has just that in mind throughout the Christian's life. As you read these words right now, the Spirit is busy developing you into the character that you are.

If drama is about resolution (a happy ending, even comedy), Christianity offers heaven instead of hell; belonging instead of isolation; hope instead of despair; and joy in the morning after a night of sorrow.

If drama is word with flesh on it, Christianity offers God incarnate, Jesus Christ, and the inspired Book of books, waiting to be put to work in life.

If drama is about symmetry between actors and audience, between symbol and reality, between the author's mind and the mind of anyone watching the drama unfold, Christianity begs for such symmetry between the mind of Christ and our own.

If drama, at its core, is about community between players and audience, Christianity is a communion of saints, communing with God, with one another, and with God's world.

No wonder scripts, actors, rehearsals, and story lines are as at home in the church as they are in the theater. No wonder that as one sings or speaks the liturgy, one senses the drama. No wonder that as one more story plays out in the sacred Scriptures, a divine drama unfolds. No wonder that as a congregation of Christians comes forward for Communion or leaves for mission or returns for prayer, it's as if it were an exit or entrance scripted in a drama.

No wonder fire, ashes, and resurrection comprise the Christian's character and costume and the church's set design.

Drama belongs in the church.

Some Tips as You Produce These Dramas

These dramas are intentionally brief. Each is designed primarily for presentation in a worship, devotional, or classroom setting. Most (with the exception of the first drama, "From These Ashes") take 6–8 minutes to present. This allows minimal rehearsal, fewer lines to memorize, and a drama that genuinely serves the Word. The following guidelines will assist in the production of the dramas.

1. **Let the dramas serve the Word.** In most cases, especially when presented in worship, the dramas assist and enhance the reading and preaching of the Word. A Scripture reference is included with each script as well as questions to encourage more thought on the drama's focus. Rarely should one of these dramas be presented with-

out a clear statement of scriptural truth. Remember, sometimes drama serves as a foil. That is, sometimes drama leaves people begging for the Gospel. At other times, drama simply raises a subject to the level of emotion or thought.

Preachers may decide to use one of these dramas immediately before or even during the sermon. Teachers may use a drama as a device to launch learners into the lesson. Some of the scripts may actually be used as an alternative method of presenting the children's message. Often children's messages ask children to make quantum leaps between concrete objects and abstract truths. Drama places divine truth before the eyes and ears of children, offering another way of understanding and responding to the Gospel.

2. **Rehearse and memorize.** Though the dramas are brief, plan at least 2 hours of rehearsal for each one. Recruit those clearly gifted for drama. Do not ask for volunteers. (Would you ask for volunteers for a vocal solo?) Be sure to get the scripts to your players early so that lines can be memorized. Reader's Theater should be a last resort (and a poor one at that since most amateur players do not have the gift for effective oral interpretation).

3. **Think about a drama troupe.** Just as a church's choral ministry works best with an organized and committed choir, drama ministry functions well with a repertoire of committed players. Consider selecting a year-long program of church drama from this and other sources to be presented by a troupe of players. The troupe can include adults, youth, and children, perhaps 12 individuals, who meet twice a month for rehearsals and encouragement.

A vital component of the troupe is a winsome, affirming director/leader whose commitment to excellence in church drama is contagious. The troupe might even function as a small group committed to Bible study and prayer and to community outreach through drama. Each of these dramas, their scriptural text foundations, and the follow-up questions provide starters for significant small-group conversations.

4. **Strive for more than bathrobes and sandals.** For many years, churches have settled for little from their drama presentations. Just as we expect excellence from our musicians and preachers, so the church has a right to expect the best drama we can give. Work on simple but striking set designs. Strive for realistic costuming. Develop characters. Mine lines for their deeper meanings. Get creative with staging the dramas. Localize certain lines if appropriate. Alter lines to be more reflective of your situation. Rehearse until excellence is achieved. Present the drama only when excellence is achieved.

5. **Do drama as ministry.** That is, do drama as service to the Lord and to others. Guard against egos taking over—forever a problem in theater (and in humanity!). Strive for fairness and equity in role assignment. Think seriously about the servanthood aspect of drama in worship and in the classroom.

6. **Celebrate life in Christ.** These dramas depict a truth that Jesus exhibited again and again—the Word of God is illustrated all around us. Life is a canvas painted with divine truth. Drama puts truth on stage. We can look at it, cherish it, participate in it, and celebrate it.

7. **Thank God for the privilege.** Those in church drama have the rare privilege of bridging the Word and life for God's people. That is no small task. It belongs to the likes of priests and prophets. Church drama places you in great company. Where the Word is, there the Spirit is as well. And where the Spirit is, there is always drama.

Repentance
and Renewal

Focus

Therefore, if anyone is in Christ, he is a new creation; the old has gone, the new has come! *2 Corinthians 5:17 (NIV)*

The Christian life moves from old to new. We change. We grow. The process can be painful. Some watch from a distance. Others refuse to march to a new cadence. Still, for those who are willing to rise from the ashes, there is hope, fellowship, and praise

Characters

Bill (playful, sincere)

Carol (warm, a bit proud, attentive)

Firefighter (official, patient)

Sam (scruffy, not well-dressed, appealing)

Elsie (arrogant, clinging to the past, stubborn)

From These Ashes

Scene

The setting is a burned-out building. A few scattered, charred beams and debris will enhance the scene. If the drama is presented in the chancel, do not use the pulpit and baptismal font. This play is especially suitable for presentation on Reformation Sunday, Ash Wednesday, during the Easter season, or for a church anniversary celebration

Bill and Carol stand center stage surrounded by charred rubble

Bill: I can't believe it. It just doesn't seem possible.

Carol: Well, believe it, Bill. You're standing in it. This is Central Christian Church—or what's left of it.

Bill: How can something like this happen? How can we be here one Sunday for worship and come the next Sunday to find our church burned to the ground? Rubble! That's all that's left.

(Firefighter wearing firehat enters; mimes shuffling through debris.)

Carol: *(Doesn't notice Firefighter)* They're not sure how it happened. Seems to me the fire department could have done more. I wonder when they arrived. I wonder if they know how much this church meant to us.

Firefighter: We did all we could, ma'am. We were here into the morning hours. I've been here all night. It's a total loss. Two firefighters are in the hospital from the smoke, you know.

Carol: I'm sorry to hear that.

Firefighter: Strange you folks should be here early on a Sunday morning.

Carol: I don't think it's strange at all. This *is* Sunday morning. We were getting ready for the 8 A.M. service, turned on our radio, and heard that a fire had destroyed our church. This *is* our church, you know. Our children were baptized here!

Bill: *(Points stage right)* Over there, near the corner of the building, that was where they were baptized. *(Walks to corner, stage right)* The font stood right here. The light would filter in through the stained-glass window over here and put a rainbow of color on the baby in the pastor's arms. Even raised a shimmer of light off the water in the font.

Firefighter: I am sorry. You really should stay clear of the area, you know. The investigation isn't complete.

Carol: This is our church, mister!

Bill: This *was* our church, Carol. *(Pauses)* The pulpit was over there. *(Walks stage left)* Has anyone called the pastor? My guess is he'd like to know about this.

Carol: This'll teach him to go on a three-week vacation! I'm sure someone has called him. What time do you have, Bill?

Bill: *(Glances at watch)* Almost 8 o'clock. *(Walks stage right as if to stand behind pulpit)* "Grace, mercy, and peace to you from God, our Father …"

Carol: Bill! Really!

(Sam enters stage left.)

Sam: Will ya' look at this! I've heard of fire and brimstone sermons, but this here's the real thing!

Bill: They burned it right down to the ground.

Sam: I can see that. Who's "they"?

Carol: Who are you? That's what I'd like to know. You're not a member of Central Christian Church, are you?

Sam: Nope. I'm not a member, but for 24 years I've been walkin' by this buildin', and I've heard some mighty fine singin'. Always thought some day I'd walk in and catch the service, as an observer, ya' understand. I never did feel you members were all that eager to have us newcomers drop by. I'll give ya' this, though, you could sing. Yes sirree, you could sure sing.

Carol: We are quite a fine singing congregation, aren't we?

Sam: Lady, if angels found themselves assembled in some corner of the earth, they'd have a hard time soundin' any better than you folks here at Central Christian.

Carol: I think I like you, ah-h-h …

Sam: Sam. The name's Sam.

Bill: This here is where the pulpit stood, Sam.

Sam: And where was the organ?

Bill: *(Points up and behind audience)* Up there. $250,000 worth of instrument up in smoke!

Sam: So who's to blame?

Firefighter: We don't know for certain. Could have been faulty wiring. These old buildings have problems deep inside that can't always be detected. That may have been the case with the church here.

(Elsie enters stage left.)

Elsie: Oh, my goodness! My goodness! Oh, my! My goodness! *Goodness me! My goodness!*

Bill: Speaking of problems.

Elsie: Bill, get down from that pulpit!

Bill: *(Looks down)* Ah, what pulpit, Elsie?

Elsie: Carol, what are we going to do? What have they done to our church?

Sam: Who's "they"? Sounds to me like you may have done it to yourselves.

Elsie: *(Glares at Sam and turns to Carol)* Who's this? He's not a member, is he?

Bill: This is Sam, Elsie. He's a neighbor.

Sam: Came to pay my last respects.

Elsie: *(Condescendingly)* How nice. Bill, get down from that pulpit! I remind you that my family bought that pulpit for this church, solid oak with imported carvings from Munich.

Bill: Elsie, I'm telling you, the pulpit is no more.

Elsie: Get on your knees, Bill Riley, and find the plaque— the one that identifies the pulpit as a gift in memory of my sainted husband, who built a good part of this church with his own two hands!

Bill: I'll not be getting on my knees to look for any plaque, Elsie.

Elsie: Confound it! Then get down out of my pulpit!

Bill: Your pulpit? I'm telling you there is no pulpit!

Elsie: *(Pulls herself together)* What are we going to do? Who could have done something like this?

Sam: Don't look at me, lady. The firefighter here says it could have been a problem inside the building.

Elsie: Nonsense. That's what they always say. I say someone else is responsible for this destruction. Someone's destroyed our church! Bill, get down from that pulpit! Carol, tell Bill to get down from that pulpit!

Firefighter: Maybe we should clear the area, folks.

Bill: Hold on, just a minute. *(Glances at watch)* By my watch, it's 8 o'clock straight up.

Elsie: So?

Bill: So, Elsie, what happens at 8 A.M.?

Elsie: Bill Riley gets down from the Goodwin Memorial Pulpit. That's what happens!

Sam: Relentless! The woman's relentless!

Carol: We'd be here for church at 8 A.M. We'd be sitting in our pews waiting for worship to begin.

Sam: I'd be out for my Sunday morning constitutional, which makes me think I oughta be on my way.

Bill: No, hold on a minute, Sam.

Elsie: He isn't a member, Bill. He can leave if he wants to. *(Turns to Sam)* Thank you, sir, for your concern. It's good to know that the neighborhood will miss our church.

Bill: *(Chants)* "O Lord, open my lips."

Carol: Bill, really.

Bill: That's what the pastor chants at 8 o'clock to start the service. *(Chants again)* "O Lord, open my lips." And what do we all sing? *(No response)* Come on, what do we sing after the pastor sings, "O Lord, open my lips"?

Sam: Everybody sings *(Sings),* "And my mouth will declare Your praise."

Elsie: How does he know that?

Sam: I've heard it every Sunday, lady, for the last 24 years— from the outside, ya' understand. *(Sings again)* "And my mouth will declare Your praise."

Elsie: Now that's amazing, truly amazing.

Sam: Truth is, ma'am, I've had a burning desire for many years to walk up those steps and join you folks.

Elsie: Did he say, "burning"? So tell us, why didn't you? The road to failure is paved with good intentions. You never did join us, did you? I've never even seen you here before.

Carol: He's here now, Elsie.

Elsie: Now doesn't count. The church is no more. It's a heap of ashes.

Sam: Like I said, maybe I should be going.

Firefighter: Maybe you should all be going.

Elsie: Find me that plaque, Bill, and quit playing preacher. I want to go home.

Bill: Elsie, you're missing the whole point.

Elsie: I am, huh! So what's the point, *Reverend* Bill?

Bill: That it's 8 o'clock on a Sunday morning, and we're here. Don't you see it? We have a great opportunity to begin again, right here, right now. "And my mouth will declare Your praise." We're still a church, Elsie, even if the building is gone.

Elsie: So?

Bill: So we start again. We rebuild.

Elsie: It won't be the same, I tell you. It won't be the same church.

Bill: No, probably not, Elsie, but we will be a church. Maybe a better church, a wiser church. We will declare His praise. Think about it. Sam, you think about it too. Will you join us?

Sam: You're soundin' more like a preacher all the time. I'll let you know.

(Sam exits.)

Firefighter: That's it, everyone. I'll have to ask you to leave.

Elsie: You fellas, look for my plaque, will you?

Firefighter: Sure enough, ma'am.

Elsie: I still say we're not responsible. Someone did this to us. You find out who! And, Bill, get down from that pulpit!

(Elsie exits. Bill steps away from pulpit area, watches Carol, who stands center stage and scans scene. Bill approaches Carol.)

Bill: What are you thinking, Carol?

Carol: If what you say is true, I'm wondering what happens next.

Bill: Something good, Carol. Something new. Something better than before.

Carol: From these ashes?

Bill: *(Exits with Carol)* From these ashes.

(Firefighter looks over scene, then exits. Curtain.)

Questions to Think About and Discuss

1. How is the church building in this drama like people?

2. What prevented Elsie from sharing Bill's hopes for the future?

3. How might this church change for the better?

4. When has pride stopped you from changing and growing for the better?

5. Do you think Sam will come back to Central Christian? What does Sam tell you about the church and its past?

6. Has God ever used a tragedy to strengthen and mature your faith?

7. What's most important about being a Christian and a church member for Bill? Do you agree with his perspective?

We Denied Him

Scene

Four costumed characters speak from four points surrounding the audience or congregation.

Scarecrow: We are the faces of denial.

Chameleon: To look at us is to see yourselves.

Scarecrow: We are not dressed in our Sunday best.

Chameleon: We have come as we are.

Scarecrow: We are dressed for denial because denial is a part of us.

Chameleon: And a part of you.

Scarecrow: We have seen ourselves.

Chameleon: And we have seen you.

Thief: We are the faces of denial.

Clown: We are a fellowship.

Thief: But we deny Him, one by one,

Clown: Singly, each with our own tremblings and truces,

Thief: Each in our own way.

Chameleon: We are chameleons, who suit our surroundings.

Thief: We conform.

Scarecrow: We bend and compromise until we fit just right.

Clown: We pretend and play roles, becoming what people want us to be rather than who we are.

Scarecrow: I play the scarecrow. I am not what I seem at all. I am an illusion, a creation born of fear. I appear to be strong, sturdy, and secure. I stand in the wind and withstand the rain. I play the scarecrow because it is important for me to look strong. I, the scarecrow, know what it is to deny Him. I denied Him the other day at school when I wouldn't share the sadness of a friend because it would have shown weakness, not strength. I denied Him too by the strong words I used at the meeting to cover up my fears.

Chameleon: We are the faces of denial. Like the scarecrow, we are not as strong as we seem. It is only the appearance of strength that we have.

Focus

A servant girl saw [Peter] seated there in the firelight. She looked closely at him and said, "This man was with Him." But he denied it. "Woman, I don't know Him," he said. *Luke 22:56–57 (NIV)*

In subtle, even modest ways, we deny our Lord. Yet as Christians, we find forgiveness for our denials by the grace of God in Jesus Christ.

Characters

Scarecrow (dressed as scarecrow with broomstick, straw, etc.)

Chameleon (wears camouflage)

Thief (wears mask)

Clown (dressed as clown)

Thief: Inside we are the ones who are afraid.

Clown: So we deny Him, the One who is true and real.

Chameleon: I am the chameleon, the one who blends the best. I am the many. I use the right words and dress appropriately for the situation. I see the right people and slap the right backs. I am right for the world. I am at home with the popular. I am comfortable with the changing mores of our times. I am tolerant, open, flexible, nonjudgmental. I am one face in a cast of thousands. I have chosen not to fight my anonymity but to make the most of it. I, the chameleon, the one in camouflage, know what it is to deny Him. I denied Him when someone turned Him into a source of ridicule. I smiled with the crowd. I blended my silent voice with the silent choir of all who have stood by and said nothing. It just wasn't the right time to speak or the right situation. So I denied Him.

Thief: We are the faces of denial. Like the chameleon, we follow the crowd and travel most often by bandwagon.

Scarecrow: Inside we know we are meant for courage, but we are afraid.

Clown: So we deny Him, the One who is true and real.

Thief: I am afraid to tell you who I am. You'll see little sign from me that my faith is real or my love sincere. If you press me for a witness, you'll find me difficult and quick to change the subject. I, with the mask, know what it is to deny Him. I play the thief and steal away His grace and heaven and give nothing in return. I would steal a bargain from the Lord and pay no price in gratitude. I wear a mask because I do not want you to know that I am His, lest you think less of me, not more. So I deny Him.

Clown: We are the faces of denial.

Chameleon: Inside we know we belong to Him, but we are afraid.

Scarecrow: So we deny Him, the One who is true and real.

Clown: I never stop laughing. I smile and dance and mime a life of total, nonstop happiness. Don't ruin the circus with children's tears or wars or cancer treatment centers. Don't quote statistics on highway deaths or child abuse. I want to laugh! *(Laughs heartily)* I, the clown, want nothing of a cross. I can hardly bear the laughter, let alone the tears. I know denial too. They offered me a cross, and I have settled for comedy. They offered me a cause. I chose entertainment. So I denied Him.

Scarecrow: We are the faces of denial. Like the clown, we pretend that all the world's a circus and a parade.

Chameleon: Inside we know that all who would come after Him must pick up a cross and follow Him, but we are afraid.

Thief: So we deny Him, the One who is true and real.

(The four gradually move center stage.)

Clown: We are the faces of denial.

Chameleon: To look at us is to see yourselves.

Scarecrow: The scarecrow.

Chameleon: The chameleon.

Thief: The thief.

Clown: And the clown.

Scarecrow: We denied Him.

Chameleon: And we will again.

Thief: Call us Peter.

Clown: Call us by any name.

Scarecrow: Call us by your name.

Chameleon: Call us Christian!

Thief: Because that is who we are and always will be.

Clown: No matter how we look or what we say or do,

Scarecrow: We are His.

Chameleon: Because with Him there is always forgiveness.

Thief: Lord, have mercy upon us.

Clown: And grant us Your peace.

(The entire cast freezes in position, then exits. Curtain.)

Questions to Think About and Discuss

1. What truths about denial did you learn from this drama?

2. Which character reminds you most of yourself, especially as you think about times when you have denied Christ?

3. According to the drama, what, more than anything else, causes us to deny Christ?

4. What is constant for Christians as we face our denials? Of what can we be certain?

God, Be Merciful to Me, a Sinner

Scene

The drama is best staged with the Tax Collector center stage, facing audience or congregation, and the Pharisee just behind. A pew or partial pew behind the characters will give the impression of a worship service. A worship leader may want to introduce the drama with some of the material above. As indicated in the script, Lent *may be substituted for* Ash Wednesday.

Tax Collector and Pharisee enter and take places center stage. Pharisee should be just over Tax Collector's shoulder.

Tax Collector: Ash Wednesday [Lent] again. We'll have a little longer confession, I'd guess.

Pharisee: We have a confession at almost every service. You'd think we could settle for once a month. Do you really want to confess your sins again?

Tax Collector: Well, it is Ash Wednesday [Lent].

Pharisee: I bet you're glad we don't use those ashes on the forehead. You don't come to church to wear your sins in front of everyone, do you?

Tax Collector: It would be a bit conspicuous.

Pharisee: I'd call it "worm" theology, cutting us down to size—getting all morbid. It's the way preachers keep business going in the church. You're not a bad person, you know.

Tax Collector: God, be merciful to me, a sinner.

Pharisee: Come on, can you really think of any sins you committed?

Tax Collector: Well, I, ah, … let me think …

Pharisee: If you have to stop to think, I'd say you're looking pretty good. Don't think too hard. Hey, if you're clean this time, take a rain check.

Tax Collector: I wasn't exactly kind to my wife yesterday.

Pharisee: Let me tell you, friend, you belong to one huge fraternity there!

Focus

To some who were confident of their own righteousness and looked down on everybody else, Jesus told this parable: "Two men went up to the temple to pray, one a Pharisee and the other a tax collector." *Luke 18:9–10 (NIV)*

Within each of us there is a struggle between Pharisee and tax collector, especially on Ash Wednesday and during Lent. Imagine a worshiper, standing for confession at the Ash Wednesday service. As he confesses his sins, he hears the whispers of Pharisaism, whispers heard throughout the church made by each of us whenever we entertain the thought that we might be too good for repentance. The whispers heard by this confessing saint have their source in the devil's temptation and in the basest of sins, the sin of pride. Remember, these are not two people, but one, contending with his or her darker side.

Characters

Tax Collector (attempts to be penitential during Lent)

Pharisee (brash, cynical, proud)

Voice from Offstage (the voice of Jesus)

Tax Collector: And there is the matter of my income tax.

Pharisee: Hey, Uncle Sam gets more than his share. He won't miss it.

Tax Collector: My language leaves something to be desired.

Pharisee: Important, sometimes, for emphasis. Shows you to be a streetwise person.

Tax Collector: I am sorry, Lord. Forgive me.

Pharisee: Okay. So you got that out of your system.

Tax Collector: God, be merciful to me, a sinner.

Pharisee: Cower, cower. So that's who you are? What about great parent? What about churchgoer? What about scout leader? What about the times you read in church and the contributions you give? How about a little mention of strengths here?

Tax Collector: Quiet. This isn't the right time.

Pharisee: The right time? If this isn't the right time, when is? You've got God's attention. Say it. Come on, say it, "I am a good person," a sight better than Jim Blodgett over there. Everyone knows the way he runs his business. And look at that hot number over there. God only knows how she found her way into a church on Ash Wednesday [during Lent]. You're a good man. Say it.

Tax Collector: God, be merciful to me, a sinner.

Pharisee: And then what?

Tax Collector: Then what? What do you mean?

Pharisee: What happens after God shows you mercy? You know He will. He always does. He's hung up on the cross. Huh, that's pretty good, isn't it? God's hung up on the cross. What happens then—after God considers the cross and forgives you again?

Tax Collector: I'll feel clean again. At peace. I'll go on.

Pharisee: And you'll sin again, won't you?

Tax Collector: Probably.

Pharisee: And because of your faith, God will forgive you again, won't He?

Tax Collector: I'm counting on it.

Pharisee: Sounds rather tedious to me. It's easier to just say you're a good person.

Tax Collector: Easier, but not the whole truth. ... God, be merciful to me, a sinner.

Pharisee: I thank You, Lord, that I am not like this guy here and all the other worms who crawl into church. At least we don't have kneelers here. It helps to keep them standing on their own.

Tax Collector: *(Falls to knees)* And grant me Your peace.

Pharisee: Oh, brother.

Tax Collector: I ask it for the sake of the bitter suffering and death of Jesus Christ, Your Son, our Lord. Amen.

Pharisee: So now he's on his knees. Where's the achiever? the persuader? the United Way volunteer? the Sunday school teacher? Where's the good guy we all know and love?

Tax Collector: Here on my knees where I belong.

Pharisee: And this will make you good?

Tax Collector: This will make me whole.

Pharisee: You won't get far on your knees, buster.

Tax Collector: To the contrary. It's where every good journey begins.

(Organ plays "Amazing Grace! How Sweet the Sound.")

Pharisee: Oh, sure, listen to that. There's no stopping them now.

Tax Collector: You can join me here, you know.

Pharisee: You won't get far on your knees. Don't you want to feel good about yourself?

Tax Collector: I'm on my way.

Pharisee: And so am I. *(Mutters to himself)* Worm theology, I tell you. Worm theology!

(Pharisee exits.)

Voice: I tell you that this man, rather than the other, went home justified before God. For everyone who exalts himself will be humbled, and he who humbles himself will be exalted.

(Tax Collector remains kneeling as a stanza of "Amazing Grace! How Sweet the Sound" is played. Congregation may sing as Tax Collector exits. Curtain.)

Questions to Think About and Discuss

1. Why do we confess our sins so often in church?

2. Have you ever struggled to think of sins you've committed? What's behind the struggle?

3. With which people are you especially judgmental? How does God's unconditional love in Jesus help you conquer these feelings?

4. In what sense do we begin every journey on our knees?

Ready or Not

Scene

Print this drama completely as a bulletin or program insert so that the congregation/audience and children can read its parts. The congregation/audience part is printed in boldface. This drama serves well as a replacement for the traditional children's message. Leader should tell children to finish the rhyme as it comes up in the story, shouting the rhyming word out loud. Following the drama, Leader or the pastor may talk with the children about the fact that Jesus' death on the cross to pay for our sins makes us ready for His second coming. You will need shoes and a coat for props.

Leader may stand to side as children gather in chancel. Characters 1, 2, and 3 enter and stand before children.

Leader: A King is coming, that's for sure,
    A King who's strong and kind and pure.
**Congregation: Ready or not, He's sure to come
    To every village, every home.**

(Character 1 enters with disheveled hair that obviously needs to be combed.)

Character 1: Hey, look at me! I'm looking good.
    I've shined my shoes, prepared some food.
    I've pressed my pants and tied my tie.
    I've even told my dog, "Good-bye!"
    I'd say I'm set. Don't you agree?
    I'm looking good. The King will see
    That I'm as fine as fine can be.
    What glory's just ahead for me!
Leader: Children, look! What's still not done?
    This funny fellow needs a *c _ _ _! (comb)*

(Character 1 exits.)

Leader: A King is coming, that's for sure,
    A King who's strong and kind and pure.
**Congregation: Ready or not, He's sure to come
    To every village, every home.**

(Character 2 enters with no shoes on.)

Character 2: Hey, look at me! I look my best!
    The King will come to be my guest.

Focus

So you also must be ready, because the Son of Man will come at an hour when you do not expect Him. *Matthew 24:44 (NIV)*

Christ wants us to be ready for His glorious return, and thanks to His redeeming work on the cross, we are ready. It's as if a king were coming to our house, and we want to look our best. God's Holy Spirit keeps us in readiness for Christ's coming as we watch, pray, repent of our sins, and attend to the things of the kingdom. Christ is coming. But some people aren't sure—are we ready or not?

Characters

Leader (pastor or worship assistant, functions as storyteller)

Congregation (congregation or audience)

Characters 1, 2, and 3 (somewhat flustered, foolish)

I look just grand, I must confess,
In my fine duds and stunning dress.
I have forgotten not a thing.
I have remembered everything.
I'll bow and maybe even sing
A song of homage to my King.

Leader: Children, look, let's tell the news:
This best-dressed woman needs some *s _ _ _ _! (shoes)*

(Character 2 exits.)

Leader: A King is coming, that's for sure,
A King who's strong and kind and pure.

**Congregation: Ready or not, He's sure to come
To every village, every home.**

(Character 3 enters with coat on backwards.)

Character 3: I have a thought, and it is true,
There's nothing left for me to do
But wait until the King comes through
And says, "How marvelous are you!"
A brand-new coat I'm wearing now
As soon before the King I'll bow.
He'll look at me and say, "That's grand!
The finest coat in all the land."

Leader: Now, children, look, I'm sure you've found
That he must turn his coat *a _ _ _ _ _! (around)*

(Character 3 exits.)

Leader: A King is coming, that's for sure,
A King who's strong and kind and pure.

**Congregation: Ready or not, He's sure to come
To every village, every home.**

Leader: Now let us see if all is done
Before the King will finally come.

(Characters 1, 2, and 3 enter with combed hair, shoes on, and coat turned around.)

Leader: Yes, hair well-combed, shoes on, coat turned 'round!
Well done, good friends! The truth you've found!

**Congregation: Ready or not, He's sure to come
To every village, every home.
Well done, good friends, well done!**

(Characters 1, 2, and 3 exit. Leader shares a few words with children. Curtain.)

Questions to Think About and Discuss

1. What do you need to straighten or clean up in your life? How will the fact of Christ's sacrifice help you overcome sinful habits?

2. If Christ came today, what would He find you doing? How does the knowledge that Christ's death and resurrection declare us ready and motivate us in our prayer and confessional life?

3. How different will you be because of the Spirit's guidance in today's worship?

4. What has the Holy Spirit helped you change in your life in response to God's Word?

Focus

In those days John the Baptist came, preaching in the Desert of Judea and saying, "Repent, for the kingdom of heaven is near." *Matthew 3:1–2 (NIV)*

John the Baptist preached not only to the lowly but to the spiritual leaders of his day, the Pharisees and Sadducees. All people come under the scrutiny of God's Law, and God calls all people, no matter how pious, to repent.

Characters

Leader (worship assistant or pastor, functions as story-teller)

Congregation (congregation or audience)

Children (say one line repeatedly as cued)

Characters 1 and 2 (bold, accusatory, even confrontational)

So Who Invited You?

Scene

Print this drama completely as a bulletin or program insert so that the congregation / audience and children can read its parts. The congregation / audience part is printed in boldface. The children's part is printed in bold italics. This drama serves well as a replacement for the traditional children's message. Leader should invite children to the chancel and quickly rehearse them to respond, "So who invited you?" when Leader points to them. The pastor may play the Pastor role and someone else play Leader. Following the drama, the pastor may talk with the children about how we are all sinners—even pastors—and in need of God's forgiveness!

Leader and children gather in chancel; Pastor stands at the pulpit. Characters 1, 2, and 3 speak loudly from seats in pews or, ideally, walk to chancel with children.

Leader: Once there was a preacher, high on a pedestal,
Everyone looked up to him; with pride his heart was full.
He was like the Pharisees in Bible days long passed—
He saw himself the first and best and everyone else last.
The people of the preacher's church were quick to give him praise:

Congregation: We've never seen a finer man in all our live-long days.

Leader: They said again as they observed his pious, saintly ways,

Congregation: We've never seen a finer man in all our live-long days.

Leader: His pedestal grew higher still as compliments were given:

**Congregation: Here! Here! The man does nothing wrong.
He's such a gift from heaven!**

Leader: The pious parson, perched atop his ever-growing tower,
Was quick to celebrate himself and said,

Pastor: I love the power!

**Congregation: Your sermons, each a masterpiece!
    Your warmth and style are grand.**

Leader: The accolades continued.

Pastor: Yes! Let's give myself a hand! *(Applauds)*
    I think that I have never seen a parson such as I,
    So gifted, kind, intelligent, and caring, humble, s-i-g-h.

Leader: And all the village people, when they saw the man
    up high,
    Shouted, all in one great voice:

Congregation: Our preacher! What a guy!

Leader: It all was rather wonderful. How lofty and how
    great
    The preacher thought himself to be, until this Advent
    late,
    A visitor appeared to say,

(Character 1 enters.)

Character 1: Your preacher I accuse!
    He's not as great as you believe!
    His pride he has to lose!

Leader: And all the people of the village shouted with dis-
    dain,

**Congregation: How dare you come among us here,
    accusing, raising cane!**

Leader: The children heard the charges too, and many, not
    a few,
    Were angry and upset. They asked,

Children: *So who invited you?*

Leader: The visitor just said,

Character 1: Well—God!

Leader: And turned and walked away.

(Character 1 exits.)

Leader: The preacher, brought down very low, just mut-
    tered, huffed, and sulked.
    Then came another visitor with much the same to say.

(Character 2 enters.)

Character 2: I saw your preacher run a red light just the
    other day.
    I also know his language can at times be very blue.

Leader: The children of the village asked,

Children: *So who invited you?*

Leader: The people scorned the visitor and said,

Congregation: It can't be true!

Leader: The children wondered once again,

Children: *So who invited you?*

Character 2: Well—God!

Leader: Said the accuser.

Character 2: And what is more, I'll say,
        Your preacher is a grumbler, and he worries every day.

Leader: And the second visitor just turned, and he too
        walked away

(Character 2 exits.)

Leader: Now everyone there wondered what their preacher
        had to say. *(Silence)*

Pastor: It's true!

Leader: He said.

Pastor: It's very true, what all of you have heard.
        I'm not the perfect person, and in fact it's quite absurd
        For me to be perched high up here, up where the air is
            thinner.
        It's time for me and you to know—your preacher is a
            sinner.

Leader: And down he came, the preacher did, down from his
        lofty height.

(Pastor comes down from pulpit and sits with children or congregation.)

Leader: On level ground he joined his friends. It was a good-
        ly sight.
        And now they say his sermons and his pastoring are bet-
            ter.
        He stops for red lights, talks clean talk, and is not such a
            fretter.
        It's good for preachers and for us to be put on alert.
        To hear the truth from those God sends—even when it
            hurts.

(Leader or pastor shares a few words with children, helping them understand that we are all sinners. Also explain that when we confess our sins, God fully forgives us because of Jesus. Curtain.)

Questions to Think About and Discuss

1. Why is it hard sometimes to think of our spiritual leaders as sinners?

2. Why is it vital for pastors to see themselves as sinners?

3. How do you think people in John's day felt about his criticism of the Pharisees and Sadducees?

4. What truth from God has been hard for you to hear? In other words, what truth hurts because you know it condemns your sin? Which words from God bring you comfort and peace?

Focus

You, dear children, are from God and have overcome them, because the one who is in you is greater than the one who is in the world. *1 John 4:4 (NIV)*

We have many options today when it comes to dealing with guilt. Christians trust that Christ, the One who is in them and with them, has overcome guilt for them. Next to faith in Christ, contemporary attempts at coping with guilt pale.

Characters

Storyteller

Man (harassed, plagued by guilt)

Shadow Figure (wears black and a black mask)

Characters 1, 2, and 3 (detached, manipulative)

Character 4 (Christ figure, warm, victorious)

The Man Who Was Very Guilty

Scene

The only prop is a pile of 25 books that can be carried.

Characters 1, 2, 3, and 4 stand with backs to audience. Storyteller stands behind scene, perhaps at lectern. Throughout drama, Man is followed, step by step, by Shadow Figure.

Storyteller: Once there was a man who was very guilty. He not only felt very guilty, but he was very guilty.

(Man enters. Shadow Figure follows.)

Man: I am very guilty. I not only feel guilty, I am guilty.

Storyteller: Wherever this very guilty man went, his guilt went with him.

(Man walks from one side of stage to other. Shadow Figure follows.)

Storyteller: Whenever he looked over his shoulder, there was his sin, just like the Bible text says, "My sin is always before me." Only this man's sin was ever behind him, haunting him, tying him to a past from which he could not break free. *(Pauses as Man and Shadow Figure pace.)* As many guilty people, this very guilty man sought rescue from his guilt.

Man: *(Still paces)* Help is what I need. I cannot go on with this *(Looks at Shadow Figure)* "thing" on my back. I need help. Help. Help. *(Notices Characters 1, 2, 3, and 4 and stops)* I wonder. Do you think …? Why not? It can't hurt to ask. *(Walks to Character 1 and taps Character 1 on shoulder.)* Excuse me.

Character 1: *(Turns to Man and audience)* Yes? May I help you?

Man: You certainly may. I definitely need help.

Character 1: What is the problem?

Man: I am guilty.

Character 1: You are very guilty. I can see your guilt.

(Notices Shadow Figure) You want relief.

Man: Oh, I do! I do!

Character 1: Your guilt is like a shadow, ever on your back.

Man: Yes, yes. You've got it. You understand. What must I do to be free of my guilt?

Character 1: You must face it. Turn and face your guilt.

Man: That's it?

Character 1: It's a start.

Man: Okay.

(Man turns and looks Shadow Figure in the eye.)

Character 1: Stare it down! Study it!

Man: Okay. *(Bears down. Shadow Figure bears down too as if in a stand off)* There. Is that it?

Character 1: Not quite. Now describe it.

Man: It's, well, it's dark and pesky and relentless, yes, relentless, and … . Are you sure this is going to work?

Character 1: There. Feel better now?

Man: Ah, no. I still feel very guilty.

Character 1: To be relieved of guilt, we need only face our guilt and describe it. Then it will be gone.

Man: Really? Mine isn't.

Character 1: Isn't what?

Man: My guilt isn't gone.

Character 1: Maybe we should try it again. Bear down more. Concentrate! Describe it more fully.

Man: I think I'll pass. Or I should say, we'll pass, my guilt and I.

(Man moves to Character 2. Character 1 turns to face away from audience. Man taps Character 2 on shoulder.)

Man: Excuse me, but I am very guilty. Can you help me?

Character 2: *(Turns to face Man and audience)* Sure. Deny it.

Man: Deny it?

Character 2: Just tell yourself you're not.

Man: Not?

Character 2: You know, not guilty. Go ahead, say it. Say it, "I am not guilty!"

Man: But I am guilty.

Character 2: You are not.

Man: Am too!

Character 2: Not!

Man: Am!

Character 2: Not!

Man: This is ridiculous. Just saying it doesn't make it so. Look! *(Shadow Figure smiles)* My guilt is still with me.

Character 2: That's because you didn't deny it.

Man: But it's here as plain as day. You mean to tell me you don't see it? *(Points to Shadow Figure)*

Character 2: I mean to tell you I don't see it. I refuse to see it.

Man: You're either blind or a mighty great pretender. I'm guilty, buster, very guilty.

Character 2: Suit yourself. He who does not deny guilt is doomed to live with it.

Man: Really?

Character 2: Really. *(Turns to face away from audience)* Loser.

Storyteller: The very guilty man's quest for relief continued. He was tenacious in seeking rescue from the shadow of past sins.

(Man goes to Character 3 and taps Character 3 on shoulder.)

Man: Pardon me, may I have a minute of your time?

Character 3: *(Turns to face Man and audience, holding books)* Certainly. I was hoping someone would come and relieve me of at least some of these books. What's the problem?

Man: I am guilty, I mean, very guilty, and I want to do something about it.

Character 3: I can recommend several titles.

Man: Titles?

Character 3: For instance, the fourth from the top. Please take it.

Man: Fourth from the top, you say? *(Fumbles to pull book from pile)*

Character 3: Yes, yes, an excellent book—*You May Feel Guilty But You're a Better Person Than Most of the People You Know.*

Man: Quite a title.

Character 3: Read it. It will help. And, oh, take the tenth one down.

Man: Tenth? Right. *(Counts down, pulls out book, and reads title)* Interesting. *Everyone's Done It, So What's the Big Deal?* Any more volumes to recommend?

Character 3: Second one from the top. Grab it.

Man: Okay. *(Takes book from pile and reads title)* Guilt *Uncovered: How Churches Use Guilt to Motivate the Masses.* Wow!

Character 3: Read them and you'll be fine.

Man: Are you sure?

Character 3: No, but that will be $64.95.

Man: $64.95?

Character 3: Not very much to pay if they work.

Man: I'll pass. *(Gives books back to Character 3)*

Character 3: Whatever. You just don't seem to grasp the genius of self-help. *(Turns to face away from audience)*

Storyteller: So the very guilty man wondered about hoping for some relief.

(Man crosses stage. Shadow Figure follows.)

Storyteller: Then it was that a gentle figure of a person turned and moved toward him.

(Character 4 turns and approaches Man.)

Character 4: I'm here.

Man: But I didn't even ask for your help.

Character 4: I heard. I can see your guilt.

Man: *(Chuckles)* Huh, so can I. What do you suggest I do?

Character 4: I suggest we conquer your guilt.

Man: We?

Character 4: I will walk with you. I'll be at your side. I'll teach you about love, about sacrifice, about forgiveness, and about life without guilt.

Man: You'll do all of that?

Character 4: That's why I've come.

Storyteller: And so it was that the very guilty man found a companion. Where he went, his new-found friend went as well.

(Man and Character 4 walk with Shadow Figure still following. Man and Character 4 mime conversation.)

Storyteller: The more they talked, the more the very guilty man learned about living without guilt. *(Shadow Figure slithers away)* Then one day, the man looked behind himself, *(Looks behind himself)* and his guilt was gone. To his amazement, when the man looked behind his new-found friend, his guilt was now behind the one who had been so kind. *(Shadow Figure slithers up behind Character 4)*

Man: I don't get it. It's my guilt, not yours.

Character 4: I choose to take it on myself,

Storyteller: Said the kind friend.

Character 4: You are free now. Forgiven. Trust me.

Man: Trust you? That's all? Trust you?

Character 4: This is why I came.

(Character 4 exits. Shadow Figure follows Character 4.)

Storyteller: And a very guilty man was not guilty anymore.

Man: Amazing!

Storyteller: He said.

Man: I trust him. I do.

Storyteller: Now, I ask you, which was the best of this man's counselors?

(Entire cast freezes in position, then exits. Curtain.)

Questions to Think About and Discuss

1. What are some faulty ways of handling guilt? Which are reflected in the drama?

2. Discuss these statements: Our guilt is not dependent on feeling guilty. We may feel no guilt but be very guilty anyway.

3. Why does it take such great trust to "lay our sins" on Jesus? Who gives us the ability to do this?

4. Why was the Christ figure in the drama the best counselor?

38

Focus

When He had received the drink, Jesus said, "It is finished." With that, He bowed His head and gave up His spirit. *John 19:30 (NIV)*

We Christians find in the death of our Savior our own death. In Baptism, we die and rise with Christ. His death counts as ours. Faith makes us one with Christ in death.

Characters

Character 1 (10-year-old child)

Characters 2, 3, and 4 (adults or youth)

Tolls the Bell— Someone's Died

Scene

Though the drama is an observed conversation, it should be done with a spirit of solemnity and wonder. The church bell may be used or a large bell from the bell choir. The bell should sound from offstage when indicated or it can be rung continuously throughout the drama. The drama may be presented as part of the Passion reading at the point when the verse announcing Jesus' death is read.

Characters 1, 2, 3, and 4 enter, talking. Bell begins to toll slowly and tolls either at the points mentioned in the script or throughout the drama.

Character 1: What's that? Did you hear it?

Character 2: It's the bell at the church. They toll it whenever someone dies.

Character 3: "Tolls the bell—someone's died." My grandfather used to say that. Wonder who it is.

Character 4: One ring per year is what they do. You can tell how old the person was by counting the rings.

(Bell tolls twice before characters speak again.)

Character 3: I lost count already.

Character 2: God knows.

Character 1: We believe that, don't we? That God knows the number of our years?

Character 2: We do. And the number of our days.

Character 3: I wonder how many rings I'll get.

Character 2: God knows.

Character 3: Wish I knew.

Character 4: Think they'll even toll the bell by the time we, ah …

Character 3: Die?

Character 4: Yeah.

Character 2: They've done it for a long, long time. It's a tradition.

(Bell tolls once before characters speak again.)

Character 3: It makes you think of time getting away from us.

Character 2: Time doesn't stop for anyone.

Character 3: Wonder if the bell is for that young father who died in the accident.

Character 4: Three children. I saw it in the paper. Tough.

Character 1: We had a neighbor die of cancer a few days ago. It could be for her.

Character 2: Hard to tell. The problem with dying is that so many of us end up doing it.

Character 3: I once heard a bell toll 108 times. 108!

Character 1: You mean somebody lived to be that old? I don't think I'd like that. You can end up pretty wrinkled by 108.

(Bell tolls once before characters speak again.)

Character 1: Think they tolled the bell for Jesus when He died?

Character 2: It's an old tradition but not quite that old.

Character 3: No, when He died, there was no bell to toll His years.

Character 1: How many times would it have tolled for Jesus when He died?

Character 4: Most say He lived to be 33. Thirty-three times.

Character 1: Not very old if you ask me.

(Bell tolls once before characters speak again.)

Character 3: Tolls the bell—someone's died.

Character 4: It is sort of an announcement, isn't it?

Character 3: With Jesus, it was thunder and an earthquake.

Character 1: Personally speaking, I like the bell a lot better.

Character 4: It's a warning too, the tolling of the bell. Like Psalm 90, the bell says, "Teach us to number our days."

Character 2: Someone's died, and someday it will toll for us.

Character 1: So when Jesus died, they just put Him away in a grave. Right?

Character 3: Right. They took Him down and put Him in a cave with a large stone rolled in front of it to seal it tight.

Character 1: Tight?

Character 3: As tight as could be.

Character 1: And no bells.

(Bell tolls twice before characters speak again.)

Character 3: I do wonder who it is that died.

Character 1: It's Good Friday, you know.

Character 2: We know.

Character 1: So maybe it tolls for all of us.

Character 4: How so?

Character 1: My Sunday school teacher says that when Jesus died, we all died.

Character 3: No, I'm sure it's for someone in town. We can walk down and see, if you like.

Character 1: I'd rather believe it tolls for us all. Yep, that's what I believe.

Character 3: But …

Character 1: No, when Jesus died, we all died. "Tolls the bell—someone's died." The bell tolls for Jesus, and the bell tolls for us.

Character 4: You really should …

Character 2: Why not let him believe what he believes? When one of us dies, something in all of us dies too.

Character 1: Yes, something in all of us died when Jesus died. Yes, that's right.

(Bell tolls once before characters speak again.)

Character 3: "With that, He bowed His head and gave up His spirit."

Character 1: And something in all of us died with Him.

Character 3: Tolls the bell—someone's died.

(Entire cast freezes in position. Bell tolls at least three more times. If the drama is presented at the point of Jesus' death in the Passion reading, the bell may toll through the remaining verses. Then entire cast exits. Curtain.)

Questions to Think About and Discuss

1. How deeply do I feel grief because of Jesus' death?

2. How have we tended to make the death of Christ unreal?

3. What does it mean to you that in Baptism we "die and rise with Christ"?

4. What needs to die in your life so that, with the Holy Spirit's guidance, you can truly live for Christ?

5. How is Christ's death a personal loss for you? a personal gain?

Faith

Whose Side Is God on Anyway?

Scene

No set design or props are necessary. Narrator may stand at a lectern or among the congregation. Characters 1, 2, and 3 stand center stage and participate in animated conversation.

Character 1 stands center stage with Characters 2 and 3 on either side.

Narrator: It's important for us to know that the Holy Spirit keeps us firm in the conviction that God is on our side. We don't want to set out on our own without being sure that God goes with us. Listen to the following conversation on just this subject.

Character 1: Did you notice how nice the weather is today?

Character 2: As a matter of fact, I did.

Character 1: That was my doing. I prayed for good weather. We had some guests coming in from out of town. I wanted their stay to be comfortable.

Character 2: And you made it happen. The good weather, I mean.

Character 1: Well, no, not exactly. I prayed for good weather. God answered. He was on my side this time, I guess.

Character 2: Your prayer determined the Midwest's weather patterns?

Character 1: I guess so. Pretty neat, huh?

Character 3: Well, wait a minute. I've been praying for some heavy rain. We need it.

Character 2: We did get a little drizzle.

Character 3: Little is right. So what does that say about my prayer? Whose side is God on anyway?

Character 1: It's pretty obvious, I think. God's on my side.

Character 3: And He's not on mine?

Character 1: Well, God can't be on both sides, can He?

Focus

Our help is in the name of the LORD, the Maker of heaven and earth. *Psalm 124:8 (NIV)*

It is good to know that God is with us to direct us and protect us. To have God on our side brings great assurance. The Holy Spirit keeps us on God's side, seeking and bowing to His will.

Characters

Narrator (sets up drama and speaks its lesson)

Character 1 (confident to the point of arrogance)

Character 2 (searching)

Character 3 (challenging)

Character 3: I guess not. But how do you know He's on your side? How can you be so sure?

Character 1: I just am. I feel it in my bones.

Character 3: Which bones? Where?

Character 1: I just know. I won. You lost. God's on my side.

Character 2: I remember how we used to pray before basketball games. The coach used to pray that God would be there with us on the court as we defeated our opponents. I used to wonder sometimes which team God was really on—especially considering the way we played sometimes.

Character 1: I always figure God goes with the winner. If you win, God's on your side. If you lose, He's not.

Character 2: That's how it works?

Character 3: I'm not sure I'm comfortable with the idea that God only stands by winners. In fact, didn't Jesus talk about losing one's life to gain it? Didn't Jesus say we could win the whole world and lose our own souls? Didn't Jesus pray in Gethsemane, "Yet not as I will, but as You will"?

Character 1: Details. God loves winners. He picks winners and stands by us.

Character 3: Us?

Character 1: Us.

Character 3: I'm sorry. I don't buy it. People get sick, get in accidents, lose their security. God's on their side as much as He's on anyone's side.

Character 2: Anyway, didn't Martin Luther say something about God being "on our side upon the plain with His good gifts and Spirit"? That sounds like God's on the side of every Christian.

Character 1: I don't see how He could be on the side of every Christian all the time. God would lose sometimes. And God never loses.

Character 2: But maybe it's not a question of winning and losing.

Character 3: Maybe we got the question all wrong in the first place.

Character 1: And what is that supposed to mean?

Character 3: Maybe the real question is not, "Whose side is God on?" but rather, "Whose side are we on?" Maybe it's more important to know we're walking with God than to claim that God wears the same color jersey we do.

Character 2: Now that's pretty heavy.

Character 1: You mean to tell me that God's as much on the side of the Chicago Bulls as He is on the side of [insert a losing NBA or local sports team]?

Character 2: The point is, being on God's side is what matters—seeking His will, knowing His will, and doing it.

Character 3: God is for all of us—win, lose, or draw. But are we all for Him?

Character 1: I'll have to get back to you on this. Anyway, it's two against one here. I'm feeling a little bit outnumbered.

Character 3: Unless, of course, God is on your side.

Character 1: The thought had crossed my mind—on a day as beautiful as this one.

Character 2: Oh, brother.

Narrator: The issue never has been, "Is God on my side?" God has proven that once and for all in Christ. The real issue is, "Am I on God's side?" So we seek His will, through His Spirit's leading, and bow to it as Jesus did when He prayed, "Yet not as I will, but as You will."

(Entire cast exits. Curtain.)

Questions to Think About and Discuss

1. What kind of prayers can a Christian say before a competitive contest? That is, what can we, in good conscience, ask from God in a win-lose situation?

2. Read Psalm 124. What is the psalmist's attitude? How does the psalmist feel toward God in this psalm?

3. Read Joshua 1:5. When God says, "I will never leave you nor forsake you," what do you think He means? What can we be sure of because of that promise?

4. In Luke 22:42, Jesus bows before His Father's will. When has accepting God's will been especially difficult for you?

5. How does St. Paul, inspired by the Spirit, describe God's will in Romans 12:2?

You May Accuse

Scene

The setting is a meeting room. Place a large table and four chairs center stage. The table and all four chairs should face the audience. When Justus is seated, he should be in the center of the table. Justus should be formally dressed, maybe even in a tuxedo. The other characters should be casually dressed, and Bud should wear a watch.

Bud, Billy, and Sarah stand center stage, facing audience.

Sarah: I don't understand who called us here or why we have to wait.

Bud: Probably a practical joke. Five more minutes and I'm history.

Sarah: *(Turns to Billy)* Sonny, don't you think you should find your parent?

Billy: Mom's outside. She'll wait. We got this letter, and it said, "Come to the Commerce Building, 12th Floor, Room 12777." It was signed, "Justus."

Bud: Yeah, yeah, kid. We got the letter too. So here we are. Now what?

Billy: I haven't been here before. *(Pantomimes looking out window)* Wow! It's really neat up here.

Sarah: I hate high places. I get sick if I look down.

Billy: What are you gonna do when you get to heaven, lady?

Sarah: Don't you worry, honey. I'll do fine. People don't get sick in heaven.

Billy: But heaven's up, and you said …

Sarah: Do me a favor, okay? No more questions.

Bud: *(Looks at watch)* My time is valuable—too valuable to waste on practical jokes. Who ever heard of Room 12777 anyway?

Billy: That's what it said right on the door—12777.

Bud: That's fine, son. I'm glad you can read.

Billy: You two aren't married or something, are you?

Bud: What's that supposed to mean?

Focus

If only there were someone to arbitrate between us, to lay his hand upon us both, someone to remove God's rod from me, so that His terror would frighten me no more. Then I would speak up without fear of Him, but as it now stands with me, I cannot. *Job 9:33–35 (NIV)*

Job wanted an arbitrator with whom he could plead his case. In the face of hard times and disappointment, many are tempted to ask for an audience with an arbitrator to accuse the Lord of injustice. Through it all, as we point the finger or shake the fist at God, He loves us and asks, as always, for continued faith.

Characters

Justus (speaks confidently)

Bud (40-year-old, bitter, angry)

Billy (11-year-old, winsome)

Sarah (argumentative, pushy)

Sarah: No, we're not married. I never set eyes on this guy until we got into this room.

Billy: I just thought the way you were so grumpy and nasty, maybe you were married—to each other, I mean.

Bud: Wrong, kid. I was married once but no more.

(Silence as Bud, Billy, and Sarah wait. Justus enters stage right with briefcase. He goes immediately, officially, behind table to chair set center stage and sits. Others move from center stage as they watch Justus.)

Justus: Fine. Sorry, I'm a bit late. Please be seated.

(Bud, Billy, and Sarah do not sit down.)

Bud: And who are you supposed to be?

Sarah: Are you an executive or something around here?

Justus: Please, be seated.

Billy: Can I call my mother first?

Justus: Please be seated, Billy.

Billy: You know my name?

Justus: We know all your names.

Sarah: We?

Billy: You sent the letter, didn't you?

Justus: We did.

Sarah: What's this "we" business?

Justus: Please be seated.

Bud: Okay, okay. Let's play along and see what this polished corporate animal is trying to peddle.

(Bud sits and the others hesitantly join him at the table.)

Justus: Now … Bud Scranton?

Bud: Yeah. So?

Justus: Sarah Potter?

Sarah: Where did you get our names?

Justus: And Billy Schmidt.

Billy: *(Raises hand)* Here!

Bud: What's this all about, mister?

Justus: The name is Justus.

Bud: So what's the deal? You haul us in here, try to impress us with this name thing, and expect us to play along with your little game. So spill it. What's your pitch?

Justus: *(Reaches into briefcase and pulls out file folder)* I have been sent to listen to your complaints.

Bud: What complaints?

Justus: I will speak plainly. Each of you has something against God.

Sarah: God?

Bud: That's right, lady, G-O-D, that benevolent deity in the sky who lets the people we love die.

Justus: You have each registered a complaint. You have accused God of treating you unfairly. You even wished out loud, like Job of old, for a chance to tell God how you feel. So I have been sent to listen to your complaints and take them before the throne.

Billy: Are you an angel or something, like in the Bible?

Justus: Something like that. *(Looks at file)* Bud Scranton. It says here that you are angry because God allowed your wife to die. You feel it is unjust. You feel God had no right—that He should have intervened and saved her.

Bud: I don't know where you get your information, but you got that one right. She should not have died. Period. She was a good woman. I loved her. God knew that. I prayed that He would pull her through, and He didn't.

Justus: The Lord has heard your complaint. *(Glances at file)* Sarah Potter. You have stopped going to church.

Sarah: I worked my fingers to the bone for that church, and I never once got a thank you. I deserved more. I thought if you go to church, live a good life, and try to be a nice person, things should go well. They haven't. God does not reward good living. I'm worse off now than when I started.

Billy: Say, Mr. Justus, are you really from heaven?

Justus: Sarah, the Lord has heard your complaint. Yes, Billy, I am. *(Looks at file)* Let's see, Billy, your complaint—I'm not sure I can find it.

Billy: Look under the Cs, like under *Computer.* I prayed for one. Not just once, but over and over again, I prayed for one. I even said I'd settle for one without a CD-ROM and the latest operating system. I got nothing. Everyone's got a computer but us. I thought prayer was supposed to work. If God's so full of love, why doesn't He give me what I want?

Justus: *(Still looks at file)* Oh, yes, 139 prayers for a computer up until last Thursday.

Billy: That's when I gave up. I figured I might as well start saving my money because God wasn't going to come through.

Justus: Billy, the Lord has heard your complaint. Is there anything else any of you would like to say? *(Closes file)*

Bud: You mean that's it?

Sarah: You just listen? Nothing more?

Billy: And now you're going to leave?

Justus: What more do you want?

Billy: I'd settle for a 386. I don't even need a printer!

Bud: Listen, if you are who you say you are, you don't surprise me at all. You come here, wow us a little bit, and then leave without giving us any answers. It figures. I'm about ready to believe this guy is who he says he is just because he hasn't given us one good answer to our complaints.

Justus: You want an answer?

Bud: Yes!

Justus: Billy?

Billy: I'd like to know why God won't give me what I want.

Sarah: I doubt if you or anyone else can make any sense out of it.

Justus: Here is the answer. It is all I can give those who accuse the Lord. No more. No less.

Bud: So say it. What's the answer?

Justus: This: *You may accuse, but God is God. He still loves you. Trust Him.*

Bud: That's it? "You may accuse, but God is God. He still loves you. Trust Him"?

Justus: That's all. I hope it is enough. *(Gathers briefcase and exits)*

Billy: Hold on, mister! If God still loves us …

Bud: Forget it, kid. He's gone. *(Walks toward exit)* And so am I.

Sarah: I'll follow you out, Bud. *(Exits)*

Billy: "You may accuse, but God is God. He still loves you. Trust Him." *(Exits)* Hey, Mom, you won't believe what just happened...

(Curtain.)

Questions to Think About and Discuss

1. In hard times, we're tempted to question God's power, God's love, or both. When have you complained to God about being treated unfairly?

2. Do you think Justus could have said more to Bud, Sarah, and Billy? If so, what more could he have said?

3. Look up these passages and identify some of the blessings that God showers on us in hard times: Romans 5:1–5; 2 Corinthians 12:7–10; and James 1:2–8.

4. How did Job, in his suffering, respond to the sovereign, all-powerful will of God? Read his response in Job 40:1–5 and 42:1–6.

5. During Jesus' suffering, He cried out to God as well. Look up Mark 15:33–34. What does it mean to you to know that Jesus Himself asked God, His Father, "Why?"

Focus

Seek the LORD while He may be found; call on Him while He is near. *Isaiah 55:6 (NIV)*

Building relationships takes time—the currency of life of which we never seem to have enough. Our relationship with God can be eroded by lack of time and energy invested in prayer, meditation, and Bible reading. God takes the initiative, though, and moves us, by His Spirit, to make time commitments to keeping our relationship with Him alive and strong.

Characters

Storyteller (engaging, teaching)

VIP (busy, suspicious, impressed with personal schedule)

Voice of God (authoritative, inviting)

The Very Important Person

Scene

VIP may sit or stand center stage. The only prop is a calendar or appointment book. The Voice of God, someone with a neutral sound and good inflection, is heard over the audio system. Storyteller may stand at the lectern or among the audience/congregation.

Storyteller: Here before us is one who could be any of us—a very important person. You can tell how important he is just by the book he has in his hands. It is a treasured book, one on which he bases his life, how he spends his time, and with whom he associates. We find him reading—his calendar [appointment book]. As he pours over the coming week, however, meticulously spending the currency of time, he has a surprise coming, a surprise we all could use.

VIP: *(Thinks aloud)* Let's see, if I make that trip on Tuesday and Wednesday, I can be back in town for Thursday's meeting. I've got to fit racquetball in too. Then there's Eric's game on Thursday night. I need to arrive at the seminar on Friday at 5 P.M. Oh, wow, this is out of hand again. God knows I need a break.

Voice of God: Yes, indeed. I know.

VIP: Pardon me?

Voice of God: I said, "Yes, indeed. I know." You said I know how busy you are, and I do. I made you. I saved you. I love you. I don't miss a move you make. I know you.

VIP: And You are?

Voice of God: I AM.

VIP: You're kidding. This is a put-on, isn't it? Maybe the office staff is up to their usual shenanigans. You're not for real, are You?

Voice of God: I AM.

VIP: Are You sure You have the right guy? I'm just your average nose-to-the-grindstone member of the rat race. Are

You sure You want to talk to me?

Voice of God: I AM, that is, if you have time for Me.

VIP: Are You kidding? This is fantastic. I didn't know You did this sort of thing anymore. Is it okay if I call my pastor? He'll never believe this!

Voice of God: Let's just leave this between us.

VIP: Right, Lord. It is okay if I call You *Lord,* isn't it?

Voice of God: That's My name.

VIP: So what can I do for You?

Voice of God: I'm glad you put it that way. I'm glad you said, "What can I do for You?" because, frankly, you have been doing quite a bit for Me.

VIP: Well, thank You.

Voice of God: Maybe it's time you allowed Me to do something for you.

VIP: All right. I could use a little divine intervention on my latest attempt at a diet. And I could also use some help with my tax situation. You know, Lord …

Voice of God: That isn't what I have in mind at the moment.

VIP: Sorry.

Voice of God: You're a very busy person, aren't you?

VIP: I am. Oops. Sorry, Lord. That's Your line. Yes, busy—very busy.

Voice of God: I've noticed that book of yours.

VIP: Yes, Lord, my calendar.

Voice of God: Valuable to you, isn't it?

VIP: One day I lost it, and I thought my whole life was in jeopardy!

Voice of God: A real treasure. I was just wondering …

VIP: Wondering? I didn't think You wondered about anything, Lord. I mean I thought You knew everything before it had to be figured out.

Voice of God: It's only an expression. That's all. For the sake of conversation, I was wondering …

VIP: Yes, Lord?

Voice of God: I was wondering if I was in your book.

VIP: *(Nervously pages through calendar)* Well, I …

Voice of God: I'm not, am I? I'm not in your book, am I?

VIP: You mean in writing, Lord? I never thought about writing Your name in, Lord.

Voice of God: I'd like you to think about writing it in now.

VIP: What would I write?

Voice of God: Try God. G-O-D.

VIP: But, ah-h-h, why?

Voice of God: Because we haven't been able to get together much lately, have we?

VIP: I have been very busy. My schedule, Lord, *(Holds up book)* look at it.

Voice of God: You have become a very important person. Very impressive.

VIP: You're not being sarcastic, are You?

Voice of God: I need to know. Am I still important to you?

VIP: Well, of course.

Voice of God: Then I'd like an appointment. I need to tell you a few things, to teach you, to guide you. So write Me in.

VIP: Well, ah-h-h, okay. Let's see. How about the day after tomorrow?

Voice of God: How about tomorrow?

VIP: Tomorrow. All right. Morning?

Voice of God: First thing.

VIP: All right. What shall I bring?

Voice of God: Your love. Your needs. Your hurts. Your Bible.

VIP: Where?

Voice of God: Wherever you want Me to be. The place is never a problem.

VIP: Home? Over coffee? First thing in the morning?

Voice of God: Home is excellent. I enjoy your home. I'll pass on the coffee though.

VIP: And what will we do, Lord?

Voice of God: We'll talk. No, I'll talk mostly. You listen.

VIP: Until tomorrow then.

Voice of God: Until tomorrow.

(VIP freezes in position as Storyteller speaks.)

Storyteller: "Seek the **Lord** while He may be found," the Scriptures teach. God wants an appointment with us. Tomorrow, even today, is not too soon to gratefully repay Him for all His love with the currency of time. That's G-O-D for those of you who have your appointment books with you.

(VIP and Storyteller exit. Curtain.)

Questions to Think About and Discuss

1. What do you think? Are you too busy? When are you too busy?

2. Is importance measured by time on a schedule?

3. How much of each week do you give to God for intentional, one-on-one communion?

4. What changes do you need to make in your schedule to make room for Christ?

Focus

When John heard in prison what Christ was doing, he sent his disciples to ask Him, "Are You the one who was to come, or should we expect someone else?" *Matthew 11:2 (NIV)*

What we need, what we're looking for, we have in Christ! There is no need to look further, and there is no need to want more. He's here with us, right now!

Characters

Leader (functions as storyteller)

Congregation (congregation or audience)

Characters 1, 2, and 3 (on the prowl, a bit off-center)

The Search

Scene

Print this drama completely as a bulletin or program insert so that the congregation/audience can read its part. The congregation/audience part is printed in boldface. This drama serves well as a replacement for the traditional children's message. Leader may be the pastor or worship assistant. Leader should tell children to finish the rhyme as it comes up in the story, shouting the rhyming word out loud. Following the drama, Leader or the pastor may talk with the children about the application of this drama. You will need a large floppy hat, wide-rimmed glasses, and a guitar.

Leader invites children to come to the chancel. Character 1, wearing hat, enters from side and looks for hat.

Leader: Once there was a woman with a great big hat.
Now what in all the world do you think about that?
She looked and she looked for the hat she had,
But couldn't find her hat!

Congregation: Now that was too bad!

Character 1: Poor me, I've looked everywhere, the whole house through.
I've checked in the closet and the hat trunk too.
I called my Aunt Sophie, asked if she might know.
I've checked the attic up and the basement down below.
No hat! Poor me! I need a hat, and quick,
Or I'll go out in the cold and get deathly sick.
So where's my hat?

Leader: The troubled woman said.
And her friends reminded her,
"It's on your h _ _ _!" *(head)*

Character 1: Oh, fiddle-dee-dee, how silly of me!

(Character 1 exits. Character 2, wearing wide-rimmed glasses, enters and looks for glasses.)

Leader: And then there was a fellow whose glasses were lost.
Upset, he shouted,

Character 2: Now where have I tossed

My glasses? I wonder if I'll ever find
My specs or maybe I'll just be blind.
Oh, no, oh, never, that'll never do!
Who knows where they are? *(Turns to children)* Do you?
   (Turns to audience) Do you?

Leader: Poor man, he wondered, and he wondered out loud.
   All his friends were looking. Said the people in the
      crowd:

**Congregation: We have no clue. We cannot solve the
      case.
   Your glasses are gone and without a trace.**

Leader: They checked every crook, every cranny, every
      space,
   Until someone said, "Hey! Look! They're on your *f _ _ _!*"
      (face)

Character 2: Oops, eh, hem! Wowee, do I feel dumb!

*(Character 2 exits. Character 3, with guitar across back,
enters and looks for guitar.)*

Leader: And then came a singer, searching near and far.

Character 3: Boo! Hoo!

Leader: Said the singer.

Character 3: It's my guitar!
   They stole my instrument! Now what will I do?
   I'll find the culprit. I'm mad! I'll sue!
   Without accompaniment I just can't sing.
   My guitar, well, it means everything!

Leader: Just like the others, with an absent mind,
   The guitarist tried hard his guitar to find.

**Congregation: We'll help you look. We'll find the crook
   Who steals guitars!**

Leader: They all were shook.
   Until someone noticed and said, "Hey! Mac!
   The guitar you want? It's on your *b _ _ _!*" *(back)*

Character 3: Oh, not to *fret!* How stupid can you get!

(Character 3 exits.)

Leader: Sometimes we're busy looking up and down;
   And all upset, we fret and frown.
   And then it hits us with a great big

Congregation: (*with a huge shout*) **Bang!**

Leader: Thank you.

Well, what do you know! We've had it all along!
It's just that way with joy and peace,
With life and love that never cease!
If we want the best and all that frees us
We have Him right here. His name is *J _ _ _!* (*Jesus*)

(*Leader or pastor shares a few words with children, helping them understand the focus of the message. Curtain.*)

Questions to Think About and Discuss

1. What do you spend time looking for when you already have it?

2. What does Jesus bring you that makes you especially happy today?

3. What makes us so quick to think we're missing something?

4. Take an inventory and celebrate what God gives you as His child!

The Woman Who Wasn't Sure about Anything

Scene

Print this drama completely as a bulletin or program insert so that the congregation/audience can read its part. You will need to divide groups that aren't sitting in readily apparent "sides." If you choose not to use the congregation/audience, recruit groups to surround Woman on her left side and right.

Woman enters and takes position center stage. Characters 1, 2, and 3 approach down center aisle.

Storyteller: Once there was a woman who wasn't sure about anything. She had these voices inside of her pulling at her, first one way and then another.

Left Side: Hello. We are the voices inside of her pulling her first one way

Right Side: And then another.

Left Side: We specialize in conflict and indecision,

Right Side: Wishy-washy-ness and double-mindedness.

Storyteller: The simplest decisions caused her major problems. She'd go to a restaurant and would be asked what she'd like from the menu.

Woman: Let's see …

Storyteller: She'd say. She liked to say, "Let's see," and she said it often.

Woman: Let's see, I think I'll have …

Left Side: Don't be too quick to order.

Right Side: Think about it.

Woman: I see you have the prime rib as a special tonight.

Left Side: Hmm, prime rib. You'll love it. You're salivating right now.

Right Side: Red meat? I thought you were giving up red meat?

Focus

Teach us to number our days aright, that we may gain a heart of wisdom. *Psalm 90:12 (NIV)*

Uncertainty can plague our days, especially if we think we have forever to make decisions. A "heart of wisdom" is never as important as when faith commitments are made.

Characters

Storyteller

Woman (indecisive, struggling)

Left Side (left side of congregation or audience)

Right Side (right side of congregation or audience)

Characters 1, 2, and 3 (should be played by children)

Woman: Maybe I'll have the, ah, … let's see …

Left Side: Go beef!

Right Side: Fish! Fish!

Woman: Ah, let's see, could you come back in a few minutes?

Storyteller: You can see how it went. So you'll not be surprised to hear her inner struggles when an inquiring mind came up and asked,

Character 1: I'm doing a survey for a class at school. May I ask you a question?

Woman: Well …

Right Side: Sure, why not, you can answer a student's question.

Left Side: Be careful. Is there a tape recorder or hidden video camera?

Woman: Well, let's see …

Left Side: Come on …

Woman: Okay, go ahead.

Character 1: What do you think about the president's economic plan?

Woman: Well, let's see. I have a very strong feeling …

Left Side: You do? Be careful. This is politics. You may make enemies here.

Right Side: You're in support of it, aren't you?

Woman: Let's see …

Left Side: How can you support all that spending?

Right Side: But the president, he needs …

Woman: Yes, yes, I have a very strong feeling, ah, both ways—I'm *for* certain things, and I'm *against* others.

Character 1: Could you be more specific?

Right Side: Yes.

Left Side: No.

Woman: No. Sorry.

Storyteller: It was the same when asked by another questioner:

Character 2: Would you like to contribute to the Homeless Children's Fund?

Woman: Well, let's see, I …

Left Side: What do you know about the Homeless Children's Fund?

Right Side: Sounds like a needy cause to me.

Left Side: You've given money to some bogus charities already. Be cautious.

Right Side: Give!

Left Side: Give a little!

Right Side: Give a lot!

Left Side: She's not made of money.

Right Side: They need it.

Left Side: She needs it.

Storyteller: And so it went.

Woman: Can I get back to you?

Storyteller: So it continued day in, day out. The woman struggled with almost every decision she faced until one day, she heard a doctor tell her, "I have to tell you. Your days are numbered." That is what he said, "Your days are numbered." He gave her the number, the number of days she had left in her life. The number is not important here. What is important is that it changed her life. She suddenly began realizing that she didn't have forever to decide, only a short time. So one day a child asked,

Character 3: What do you think of Jesus Christ?

Storyteller: In the past she had hemmed and hawed, went this way and that.

Woman: Let's see …

Storyteller: She'd say.

Left Side: Be careful, they'll get you in a church and on a committee.

Right Side: You've always liked the stories and the hymns.

Left Side: Don't commit. Save it for later.

Storyteller: But this time she said,

Woman: I believe.

Left Side: "I believe"? You do? Hold on …

Right Side: This is a bit quick.

Left Side: *(Turns to Right Side)* See what you did now? You pushed.

Woman: I believe … and it's time I said so. I don't have forever. Jesus is the Son of God and my Savior. He lived for me and died for me.

Storyteller: And that was that! Who knows? Maybe now we'll even see her ordering off menus and having opinions on politics and giving to charities. The moral of the story? That's easy.

Left Side: It is?

Right Side: Are you sure?

Left Side: Maybe you should think about it.

Right Side: We should be consulted, you know.

Storyteller: The moral of the story is this: None of us has forever—especially when it comes to the question:

Character 3: What do you think of Jesus Christ?

Storyteller: It's important to speak up—now—while we have time.

(Entire cast exits. Curtain.)

Questions to Think About and Discuss

1. Do you tend to live as if you'll never die?

2. What does "numbering our days" mean to you?

3. Why are we so slow in making some decisions?

4. What difference would it make to your life if you knew how many days you had left to live on earth?

5. Does our church present the Gospel of Jesus Christ with a sense of urgency? Explain.

6. Should every service present the Gospel? Explain.

7. Spend a moment in prayer, thanking Christ, your Savior, for your eternal relationship with Him.

Hope

The Woman with the Sign

Scene

Storyteller may be stage right, among the congregation/audience, or at lectern behind the action. The impact of the drama depends on Characters 1, 2, and 3 moving as directed through the script because they play a variety of roles. You will need a large sign on a wooden picket that reads, Where is God in this? *You will also need three chairs.*

Characters 1, 2, and 3 take positions center stage.

Storyteller: Once there was a terrible accident. Cars were bent and damaged. What's worse, people were damaged too. As is often the case, people gathered to see the event unfold. They could be heard saying:

Character 1: A real tragedy.

Character 2: A lesson for us all.

Character 3: There but for the grace of God go I.

Storyteller: And suddenly, a woman entered the scene. *(Signbearer enters.)* She was holding a sign, and the sign read, "Where is God in this?" The woman did not receive a kind reception. One of the people standing nearby whispered,

Character 2: One of those strange sorts. You never know where they'll show up.

Character 1: She probably holds up John 3:16 signs at sports events too.

Character 3: She should not be here,

Storyteller: One of them said, implying that the woman and her sign were in very poor taste. Then the very same person asked the woman,

Character 3: What does God have to do with this?

Storyteller: It was the woman's question in different words. The woman remained for a time. When someone asked her,

Character 2: What do you mean, coming here with that sign?

Focus

But now, this is what the LORD says—He who created you, O Jacob, He who formed you, O Israel: "Fear not, for I have redeemed you; I have summoned you by name; you are Mine. When you pass through the waters, I will be with you."
Isaiah 43:1–2 (NIV)

When hard times hit, we long to be assured that God is present. No matter how difficult the challenge, we want to know for sure that we are not alone, that we are loved

Characters

Storyteller (animated, engaging, wise)

Signbearer (mysterious, look of longing)

Characters 1, 2, and 3 (play a variety of roles, will need coats or jackets)

Storyteller: She only said,

Signbearer: It's just a question. Maybe you can help. Where is God in this? I want to know.

Storyteller: But there was no answer—only stares. So the woman left.

(Signbearer exits. Characters 1, 2, and 3 sit on chairs stage left.)

Storyteller: Not long after this, three people at a hospital waited for news of their loved one. Surgery was taking place. It was cancer, they had been told. Now they waited. They were afraid, uncertain, and thinking the worst. And, you guessed it, *(Signbearer enters and stands behind Characters 1, 2, and 3)* in walked the woman with her sign in hand, "Where is God in this?" First, there was silence, then confrontation.

Character 3: We do not appreciate your sign,

Storyteller: One of them said.

Character 2: This is no place for protests or demonstrations or whatever it is you think you're doing.

Storyteller: The woman with the sign only said,

Signbearer: It's only a question. Maybe you can help? Where is God in this? I want to know.

Character 1: You are wrong to be here. This is a real tragedy.

Character 2: A lesson for us all.

Character 3: There but for the grace of God go I.

Storyteller: That is what they said. The woman had heard it before. Now she heard it again.

(Signbearer exits. Characters 1, 2, and 3 move stage right, put on coats or jackets, and stand in straight line, facing stage left.)

Storyteller: One night soon after, almost 100 homeless people were standing in line to receive a free Sunday supper. It was cold outside. Some shivered. All were waiting for the doors to open. Standing in line, they said,

Character 2: Will we get in tonight?

Character 1: We always get in. They'll have enough.

Character 3: They always do. *(Characters 1, 2, and 3 face forward.)*

Storyteller: And those who sat in their cars, waiting impatiently for the stoplight to change, said to one another as they looked at those in line,

Character 1: A real tragedy.

Character 2: A lesson for us all.

Character 3: There but for the grace of God go I.

(Characters 1, 2, and 3 stand in line and face stage right. Signbearer enters.)

Storyteller: And, sure enough, there was the woman with the sign again. And the homeless people in line for their supper read the sign and said,

Character 1: Good question, lady.

Character 2: If you find out, let me know.

Storyteller: And one of them said,

Character 3: Listen, lady, God don't stand in line for nobody. He ain't in this line with us. That's for sure.

Storyteller: And that was about as close as the woman came to getting an answer to her question. It's only a question, she told them.

Signbearer: Maybe you can help. Where is God in this? I want to know.

(Entire cast freezes in position while Storyteller speaks.)

Storyteller: And there is a lesson from our story. When things are bad and the sky is black with storm clouds rolling in, when bad things happen to good people, when we see a world of sadness, hurt, and pain, then we can say what others have said, "A real tragedy. A lesson for us all. There but for the grace of God go I." Or we can ask, deep from our hearts, the question the woman with the sign asked, "Where is God in this?" And we can hope to heaven that someone close will remind us: God is right here, beside us, above us, around us, and before us.

(Entire cast unfreezes. Signbearer speaks as she moves through the audience. Characters 1, 2, and 3 watch as Signbearer exits and then they exit.)

Signbearer: It's only a question. Maybe you can help. Where is God in this? I want to know.

(Curtain.)

Questions to Think About and Discuss

1. When is it hard for you to recognize God's presence?

2. What blurs or clouds God's presence for you?

3. What do you think Jesus meant in Matthew 5:8, "Blessed are the pure in heart, for they will see God"?

4. Jesus felt forsaken during His suffering on the cross, yet He died for us, praying, "Father, into Your hands I commit My spirit" (Luke 23:46). What do those words tell you about the relationship between Jesus and His Father? What hope do they offer suffering Christians?

5. During what difficult time have you been blessed to know the rich, empowering presence of God?

Going Up

Scene

Characters 1, 2, and 3 are strangers on an elevator. They stand center stage, facing the congregation. No props or set design are necessary. Miming actions, such as pressing the floor buttons, should be well-rehearsed.

Character 1 stands center stage, looking up as if at the floor indicator on an elevator, then looks straight ahead as if the door has opened. Character 2 enters and stands next to Character 1.

Character 2: Ah, could you press 24, please?

Character 1: Sure. (*Pantomimes pressing button*)

Character 2: Thanks.

(*Characters 1 and 2 "ride" in silence, then look straight ahead as if the door has opened. Character 3 enters and stands in front of Characters 1 and 2.*)

Character 3: Going up?

Character 1: Sure are.

Character 3: Great. (*Stands next to Characters 1 and 2*) Would you mind pressing 44, please?

Character 1: You bet. (*Pantomimes pressing button*) You sure are going up. What's up on the 44th?

Character 3: Corporate offices of Computronics, Inc.

Character 1: (*Nods with familiarity*) Hmm.

Character 2: I'm going up higher than that.

Character 1: I thought you said 24?

Character 3: Anyway, 44 is the top floor. You can't go any higher than that.

Character 2: I'm going to heaven.

(*Characters 1 and 3 glance at each other doubtfully.*)

Character 1: I see. We're happy for you.

Character 2: (*Turns to Character 1*) Are you going to heaven?

Character 1: I don't even know you. How can you ask me if I'm going to heaven?

Focus

But you are a chosen people, a royal priesthood, a holy nation, a people belonging to God, that you may declare the praises of Him who called you out of darkness into His wonderful light. *1 Peter 2:9 (NIV)*

Those on the way up and those who have just hit bottom need to hear Christians share the news of the amazing grace of God. The Gospel—told by Christians in fulfillment of their life's purpose—brings a song to those in darkness.

Characters

Character 1 (intense, skeptical, pressured)

Character 2 (unabashed, conversational evangelist)

Character 3 (professional, polished)

Character 2: You either are or you aren't. Which is it?

Character 1: I'm going to the 40th floor, okay? I don't discuss ultimates with strangers. Anyway, here comes the 24th. Don't you get off here?

Character 2: I think I'll just ride up with the two of you.

Character 1: Peachy.

Character 2: *(Turns to Character 3)* So how about you? Are you going to heaven?

Character 3: I suppose I am.

Character 2: How do you know?

Character 3: I guess I've lived a pretty good life.

Character 2: So you're going to heaven because you've been a good person?

Character 3: Sure. Whatever.

Character 2: What if you haven't been good enough?

Character 3: Excuse me?

Character 2: What if the entrance requirements ask for more than just being good?

Character 3: I'll just have to trust that whoever is at the gate will allow mercy to override justice.

Character 2: Oh, so you need mercy to get in?

Character 1: Hey, this is getting too deep for me. We're almost to 40—where I get off.

Character 2: Why don't we take another ride down and up again—the three of us? What do you say?

Character 1: Three strangers riding up and down on an elevator, talking about heaven. What is life coming to?

Character 2: Why not?

Character 1: It's ridiculous.

Character 2: Aw, come on.

Character 1: Who are you, anyway, some sort of elevator evangelist? I'm waiting to hear "Amazing Grace!" come over the speaker up there *(Points up)*. Here's the 40th. *(Hesitates exiting and turns to Character 3)* If you ride, I will.

Character 3: Sure. Why not?

Character 2: Great. *(Turns to Character 3)* So you need mercy. *(Turns to Character 1)* How about you?

Character 1: I need peace. If heaven is a place where things finally settle down, I'm interested.

Character 2: Life has its ups and downs, doesn't it?

Character 3: Very funny. A real punster. Here's the 44th. *(Hesitates, then pantomimes pushing button)* Okay, here we go. Down to 1.

Character 2: More ups or downs?

Character 1: What's that?

Character 2: Does life have more ups or downs for you?

Character 1: Lately more downs.

Character 2: I'm sorry.

Character 3: Me too. Wow, this thing goes down fast. We've hit bottom already.

Character 1: I know the feeling.

Character 3: *(Pantomimes pushing buttons)* Let's see, 24, 40, and 44. Here we go.

Character 1: *(Turns to Character 2)* And what about you? How will you get into heaven?

Character 3: He'll probably talk his way in, the way he persuaded us to take this little elevator ride.

Character 2: No, God has promised me heaven and provided the way in Jesus Christ, who took my punishment for my sins. I believe, and so it will be.

Character 1: You're very fortunate to have such faith.

Character 2: It's sort of like getting on an elevator, trusting that it works, and finding out, as the doors open to your destination, that it does. Sort of like, well, this. Here's my floor—24. You see, it worked. *(Character 2 exits)*

Character 3: That's it? You're getting off?

Character 2: I am.

Character 3: No hard sell? No make a commitment?

Character 2: Nope. See you again, I hope.

Character 3: A strange character.

Character 1: Confident, though.

Character 3: I haven't thought about heaven for a long time.

Character 1: I suppose it's hard to think of heaven when you think you're already at the top—or when you've hit the skids for that matter.

(Characters 1 and 3 "ride" in silence, then Character 1 begins whistling "Amazing Grace! How Sweet the Sound." Continues whistling through third line.)

Character 3: What's that tune you're whistling?

Character 1: Oh, nothing. Here's the 40th. See you again.

(Character 1 exits, whistling third line of "Amazing Grace! How Sweet the Sound.")

Character 3: Right.

(Character 3 stands alone, silently, then exits, whistling last line of "Amazing Grace! How Sweet the Sound." Curtain.)

Questions to Think About and Discuss

1. It's incredible to many how ready some Christians are to talk about their faith—even with strangers. What makes many of us hesitant to do the same thing?

2. Do you think the "elevator evangelist" was too pushy, too intrusive?

3. Talk about the comment, "It's hard to think of heaven when you think you're already at the top." Look at Jesus' comments on the issue in Matthew 19:23–24.

4. If someone were to ask you, "How will you get into heaven?" how would you respond?

Focus

"Men of Galilee," they said, "why do you stand here looking into the sky? This same Jesus, who has been taken from you into heaven, will come back in the same way you have seen Him go into heaven." *Acts 1:11 (NIV)*

Christians look to heaven. We know Christ will come again in glory. Our look heavenward, though, must never stop us from seeing life and love on earth

Characters

Storyteller (animated, enthusiastic)

Woman (colorfully costumed)

Characters 1 and 2 (skeptical, harshly judgmental)

The Woman Who Kept Looking Up

Scene

No set design is necessary. Storyteller may stand behind the action, at a lectern, or among the congregation.

Woman stands stage left, head raised, looking up. Characters 1 and 2 stand stage right.

Storyteller: Once there was a woman who was always looking up. Her looking up was noticed by those around her.

Character 1: There she is, the woman who is always looking up. You've heard about her, haven't you?

Character 2: Who hasn't? Everyone has heard about her. After all, she is quite conspicuous.

Character 1: What do you think she's looking at?

Storyteller: That was the question everyone finally asked about the woman, "What do you think she's looking at?"

Character 2: I don't think she's looking at anything. She must be looking *for* something.

Character 1: What makes you say that?

Character 2: Well, take a gander. What's up there to look *at?*

Character 1: Sky. Maybe she's a weather watcher—or a birdwatcher. Maybe she's been hired by some atmospheric study commission to watch the air currents or something.

Character 2: Give me a break. She looks snooty if you ask me, downright snooty.

Character 1: Could be she was born that way. Or maybe it's a disability. It could be she just has a stiff neck.

Character 2: *(Sarcastically)* Sure. "Oh, ye stiff-necked people, repent, for the kingdom of God is at hand!"

Character 1: Has anyone ever asked her? I mean, come right out and asked her?

Character 2: Probably not. Would you like to have a conversation with the likes of her? You have to admit, she's lacking in eye-to-eye contact.

Character 1: Go ahead. Ask her.

Character 2: You ask her.

Character 1: Okay, I will. *(Walks over to Woman)* Excuse me. *(No response)* I said, excuse me.

Woman: *(Continues looking up)* Yes, what is it?

Character 1: Well, I was wondering …

Woman: Yes, please, say it.

Character 1: I was wondering …

Woman: You are wondering why I am looking up.

Character 1: Exactly.

Woman: Many people wonder about that.

Character 1: Well, why are you? *(No response)* I asked, why are you looking up? *(No response)*

Character 2: Give it up. She's gotta be a whacko.

Character 1: A very strange person. *(Returns to stage right)* A very strange person indeed.

(After a brief silence, Woman turns and looks right at Characters 1 and 2.)

Woman: I am neither stiff-necked nor whacko. I am waiting to see what happens next. And that is all I'm going to tell you. *(Looks up again)* Now, if you'll excuse me.

Character 1: What does she mean, "waiting to see what happens next"? Next after what?

Character 2: Who knows? I still say she may not be playing with a full deck. Her elevator may be stuck between floors.

Character 1: Really. You don't have to be cruel.

Character 2: Listen, you can defend her all you want, but as I see it, she's missing what's here while she waits for whatever it is that's up there. She's missing life, living, loving.

Character 1: I guess you're right. A shame, though. Someone could offer her a handshake or a hug or a rose or a gift and she'd miss it.

Character 2: You've got that right. So let's go.

Character 1: Okay.

(Characters 1 and 2 exit.)

Storyteller: And still the woman kept looking up. She's still looking up today, waiting for the next thing to happen. Some say she's one of those who thinks so much of heaven that she's no earthly good. Others say she reminds them that there is something very big on the horizon and we had better be ready when it comes. She's not the first, you know, to gaze up into heaven, and she will not be the last.

(Curtain.)

Questions to Think About and Discuss

1. What disturbs you about the woman who kept looking up? What do you like about her?

2. What's good about looking forward to heaven? What's dangerous about it?

3. Do you think the two onlookers could have done more as they confronted the woman?

4. As Christians, what does our look toward heaven mean for our life on earth? In other words, how does earth benefit from our awareness of heaven?

5. Do you look forward to Christ's return? Explain your response.

Focus

We continually remember before our God and Father your work produced by faith, your labor prompted by love, and your endurance inspired by hope in our Lord Jesus Christ. *1 Thessalonians 1:3 (NIV)*

Christian hope, rooted in Christ, empowers Christians to endure and to persevere under pressure in the present tense. Our tomorrow is a promise of God, filled with opportunities to give Him praise and service.

Characters

Storyteller (colorfully costumed, reads from large storybook)

Clockmaker (bearded, gentle)

Wife (nagging)

Child (whining)

Town Clerk (official, well-dressed)

Customer (complaining, threatening)

Apprentice (bumbling, nervous)

The Clockmaker Who Had Tomorrow

Scene

Two clocks are necessary for staging the drama. Both clocks should be large enough to serve as central visuals in the action. One keeps time and can be heard as it ticks. The other has no hands and does not tick. As the drama opens, only the working clock is seen center stage. You may wish to design the set and costumes to reflect an alpine village. The play is especially suitable for New Year's celebrations.

Storyteller sits on stool stage right and holds a large storybook. Large ticking clock is center stage.

Storyteller: Once there was a clockmaker whose job it was to make and repair all the clocks in his village.

(Clockmaker enters and inspects clock center stage.)

Storyteller: A good many clocks there were in his village too, for this was a town that took its time very seriously. The clockmaker was kept very busy. At the center of the town there stood the great town clock that ticked away and reminded everyone in the village that time was running out. Soon another day would pass, and night would come, and that was that. No wonder, then, that the clockmaker had his hands full—and his ears too. Everyone wanted a piece of time, including his wife.

(Wife enters stage right in a hurry.)

Wife: Listen, old man, as best you can because I don't have all day.

Clockmaker: I beg your pardon, dearest wife, but that is exactly what you have—all day.

Wife: Don't be smart. I'll have you know that chores pile up at home while you tick-tock your way across the town. The house needs paint, and the woodpile's down. The wagon wheel's not right, and I have a hunch there's a mouse in the house. So will you get it all done before the clock's run out?

(Wife exits stage left.)

Clockmaker: I'll do my best, dear wife. It's all that I can do to make and keep the time clocks right.

Storyteller: The man's own kin could turn on him. His child was not much better.

(Child enters stage right.)

Child: Oh, Father, give it up. There must be something else to do beside this tick-tock business. They laugh at me at school and call me names. They ask, "How's Father Time?" So quit the business, Daddy dear, before the day is through.

(Child exits stage left.)

Storyteller: The man had hoped his trade brought home the bread and butter—and some pride too. What he found was shame instead. While he worked on the village clock, the town clerk came and said,

(Town Clerk enters stage right.)

Town Clerk: Excuse me, sir, but we need your payment in full. You've paid no taxes yet this year, and time is running out. Pay in full or go to jail!

Clockmaker: I'll do my best. I know I owe.

Town Clerk: Just fix the clock and don't expect the village to pay your bill until you pay the village what you owe!

(Town Clerk exits stage left.)

Storyteller: Some days, you see, people parade before us, making claims on time and money.

(Customer enters stage right, carrying a small clock. Customer points to the clock face.)

Customer: So it's 1 o'clock in the morning, is it? And the sun's right overhead! This clock's no good since your repair, and I'll leave it with you just one day, until tonight. You fix it right this time or I'll have my money back!

(Customer exits stage left.)

Clockmaker: I'll do my best.

Storyteller: He did his best, the old man did. He always did his best. But things came harder still because his apprentice was anything but skilled.

(Apprentice enters stage right carrying clock parts—gears, springs, hands.)

Apprentice: Say, boss, where's the clock that fits these parts? Can't find it anywhere. I wonder if you'd mind if I'd just watch again. My fingers and my thumbs are all mixed up.

Clockmaker: Just do your best. It's all that we can do.

(Apprentice exits stage left.)

Storyteller: Each day seemed harder than the one before, until one day the clockmaker disappeared.

(Clockmaker exits stage right.)

Storyteller: The villagers missed him, sure enough. He was, after all, a man of some importance, but one with too many pressures. Some thought he had died from all the various clocks he kept. But what he did instead was this.

(Clockmaker enters stage right with clock without hands.)

Storyteller: He made himself a clock that would stand in the village square next to the other great clock the town called theirs. Only this clock would have no hands. It would not tick. And it would not tock. He called it the Tomorrow Clock. *(Entire cast enters stage left)* Those in the village protested when they saw it.

Wife: I think the man has lost his wits!

Child: Oh, Father, what will they call me now?

Customer: Hmm! It works no better than my clock did!

Apprentice: I'd say something's missing, wouldn't you?

Town Clerk: Time is running out, my friend.

Storyteller: But there in the village square, the clockmaker smiled. From that day on, in the press of time, when people brought him their demands, he would only say,

Clockmaker: I will do my best. I have today, but I also have tomorrow.

Storyteller: He'd look at his Tomorrow Clock and smile and say,

Clockmaker: If not today, then tomorrow, for sure.

Storyteller: The old man said that tomorrow had become

his friend. It was for him a day without a minute spent as yet, a promise sent from God.

(Entire cast freezes in position, then exits stage right and left. Curtain.)

Questions to Think About and Discuss

1. Why did the clockmaker need his Tomorrow Clock?

2. What excites you most about your tomorrow (your future)?

3. What has Jesus promised you about tomorrow? *(See John 14:1–6.)*

4. As you think about today and all you have to do, what is most important? *(See John 9:4.)*

5. What is true about today, tomorrow, and every day? *(See Hebrews 13:8 and Psalm 31:15.)*

6. What makes you anxious and worried today?

7. What advice does God offer in 1 Peter 5:17?

Focus

Therefore, since we are surrounded by such a great cloud of witnesses, let us throw off everything that hinders and the sin that so easily entangles, and let us run with perseverance the race marked out for us. *Hebrews 12:1 (NIV)*

As we run the race of faith, the voices in the cloud of witnesses cheer us on. Perseverance means running with our "eyes fixed on Christ" for as long as it takes.

Characters

Storyteller

Running Man (dressed in warm-ups, out of breath)

Reporter (holds microphone)

Voices (can be voices of congregation or of children)

Running Man

Scene

Running Man should be dressed in warm-ups, clearly in the middle of a race. Quickly rehearse the congregation/audience before beginning the drama. An (×) represents a clap. Reporter should use a microphone if possible.

Storyteller speaks from the lectern or among the congregation. Running Man enters from behind audience after first sentence and jogs around the audience.

Storyteller: Once there was a man who ran, and ran, and ran. He was known simply as the running man in his town. Periodically, he would set out running for long periods of time. Not long ago, he had been running for three days straight. Naturally, this drew the interest of the local media, one member of which encountered the man on the street.

(Running Man runs near Reporter, who stops him. Running Man continues to run in place throughout interview.)

Reporter: Excuse me.

Running Man: Yes, what can I do for you?

Reporter: I see you're on the run again.

Running Man: That's very observant. Let me congratulate the media on another fine piece of reporting. Worthy of a Pulitzer!

Reporter: Thank you.

Running Man: What do you need?

Reporter: Will you answer a few questions?

Running Man: Sure. Shoot.

Reporter: What are you running for?

Running Man: Would you believe the U.S. Senate?

Reporter: Well …

Running Man: Just kidding.

Reporter: Seriously, why do you run?

Running Man: Well, I'm not sure. Once in a while I get this urge to take off running.

Reporter: But, Running Man, you've been running for three days now. When will you stop?

Running Man: When it's time to stop.

Reporter: Do you have a destination? Are you running anywhere in particular?

Running Man: Excuse me?

Reporter: Is there a finish line?

Running Man: I hope so. But the challenge of the run is plenty; I don't think much about the finish.

Reporter: You run alone, don't you?

Running Man: Usually.

Reporter: So there is no real competition, is there?

Running Man: Competition?

Reporter: You're not running against anyone, are you?

Running Man: I suppose not. Why do you ask?

Reporter: I thought maybe competition would keep you going. You know, winning.

Running Man: No.

Reporter: What does keep you going? I mean, how do you keep running for so long? Don't you get so tired you could drop?

Running Man: Sometimes, but it's then that the voices kick in.

Reporter: The voices?

Running Man: You think I'm strange, don't you?

Reporter: Well …

Running Man: You think I'm some tree-huggin', granola-munchin', communer-with-nature type who hears strange voices.

Reporter: Well … ah … you have to admit, hearing voices usually sends up a red flag. Tell me about these voices.

Running Man: They are … just voices. When I'm almost ready to drop, when I think I can't go one step farther, the voices come, and they say …

Reporter: Yes, they say … what do they say?

Running Man: Nah … you'll just laugh.

Reporter: No, please, I want to know. When you're almost ready to drop, the voices come, and they say ...

Running Man: The voices say,

(Storyteller signals congregation as rehearsed.)

Congregation: Don't quit! (×)(×) **Hang on!** (×)(×) **I'll give you what you need.**

Reporter: Do you think the voices speak for God?

Running Man: I do.

Reporter: What is it they say again? They say:

Congregation: Don't quit! (×)(×) **Hang on!** (×)(×) **I'll give you what you need.**

Reporter: And that's what keeps you going?

Running Man: That's it.

Reporter: Amazing.

Running Man: Now I need to get going. *(Starts to run away)*

Reporter: But how long will you keep running this time? It's been three days.

Running Man: As long as it takes. Yes, as long as it takes. See ya!

(Running Man exits running.)

Reporter: *(Turns to congregation)* Now what does he mean by that—"as long as it takes"?

Storyteller: And Running Man was off again—running. He understood that it would be easy to quit—were it not for the voices cheering us on with the counsel of God. To us too the Word comes when we need endurance. God says:

Congregation: Don't quit! (×)(×) **Hang on!** (×)(×) **I'll give you what you need.**

Storyteller: For as long as it takes!

(Entire cast exits. Curtain.)

Questions to Think About and Discuss

1. How aware are we of those who have gone before us in faith?

2. When we get fatigued and stressed in our run through life, what sustains us?

3. How do you understand the phrase in the drama, "for as long as it takes"?

4. Who carries the Word of God to you when you need encouragement?

Focus

My soul waits for the Lord more than watchmen wait for the morning, more than watchmen wait for the morning. *Psalm 130:6 (NIV)*

Each character in the nativity of our Lord was waiting, just like every worshiper at Christmas. We wait for the story to unfold and for the unique blessings of the incarnation in our lives. We wait, and the Lord comes.

Characters

Mary

Joseph

Shepherd

Wise Man

Characters 1 and 2 (bridge the scene to audience or congregation)

Watchers in the Night

Scene

This drama is most suitable for presentation on or near Christmas Eve, especially for a candlelight service. Each character could hold a candle. Use period costumes for the nativity characters. Work hard at authenticity (forget the bathrobes!). Characters 1 and 2 may dress in bright Christmas colors or white albs. Characters 1 and 2 may be the worship leaders. Position the nativity characters around the front of the sanctuary or worship site. (They can move to a microphone in larger settings.) Characters 1 and 2 may frame the scene. After each nativity character speaks, he or she moves to center stage and takes position in the Christmas tableau. A manger and wooden outline suggesting a stable will enhance the scene. Some characters kneel; others stand. Memorize all parts and rehearse carefully and completely. Few roles are more challenging in drama than a single-character monolog.

Entire cast enters and takes positions. Characters 1 and 2 move to speaking positions.

Character 1: We are all watchers in the night.

Character 2: We wait, and we watch.

Character 1: We watch from the darkness for the light that is to come.

Character 2: Joseph was a watcher in the night.

Joseph: I watched to see if the dream would come true. An angel had said that my Mary would bear a Son, the Promised One, the very Son of God. His name would be Jesus for He would save His people from their sins. In the silence of that night, I watched to see if God-given dreams and God-given promises would come true.

Character 1: If you perhaps cling to a dream, trying to understand the promises of God in a world of disappointment, then you are like Joseph, a watcher in the night.

Character 2: If you have yet to make sense of an inkling, to declare real what is imagined and hoped for, then in the watchnight of Christmas, keep watching, for your light will come.

Character 1: Mary was a watcher in the night. Listen.

Mary: I watched as the events unfolded and treasured them all in my heart. I watched, and God did what God had promised, but as I watched, I wondered. This Child, what would His future hold? What sorrows would be His as He fulfilled His destiny? The mystery of it held me captive as the Promised One lay in the manger.

Character 2: If for you the Gospel is more mystery than news, if you live with questions and wonderings sometimes too deep for words, you are like Mary, a watcher in the night.

Character 1: If you have deep concerns for the future—wondering where it all leads, this parade of events we call life—then in the watchnight of Christmas, keep watching, for your light will come.

Character 2: One whose business it was to watch in the night was a shepherd from the hills near Bethlehem, who, as the story goes, had been "keeping watch over his flocks by night."

Shepherd: It was for me a night like any other night—quiet with not much more than the sounds of the flock. I expected little. There were times, late in the night, when I watched the flock with one eye open and the other shut. That is what is so marvelous to contemplate—how ordinary was the night.

Character 2: If for you this Christmas Eve—here and now—is no more than an ordinary night, if your life of late has been a matter of doing business with one eye open and the other shut, you are like the Christmas shepherd, a watcher in the night.

Character 1: If you have been watching for a long time only to see what is less than memorable, less than passion-arousing, less than you ever thought life would be, then in the watchnight of Christmas, keep watching, for your light will come.

Character 2: And who gazed more intently into the night sky than the Wise Man, who knew the sky well enough to see a miracle unfolding.

Wise Man: We saw the star and knew. Where it went, we would follow. But to where and to whom? And for how long? And what of Herod with his murderous designs? And when is enough? When do you turn back and call it a legend? We did ask questions as we followed. We wondered aloud as we followed the star.

Character 2: If you have been following Christ for a very long time, packing along all your doubts as well, if you have considered it at times not much more than a legend, you are like the Wise Man, a watcher in the night.

Character 1: If you need some reassurance that you took the right road when the Spirit led you to Christ, that at the end there is truth and the kingdom, then, in the watchnight of Christmas, keep watching, for your light will come.

Character 2: We are watchers in the night.

Character 1: As it was in the beginning, is now, but need not be forever.

Character 2: Keep watching.

Character 1: Your light will come.

Character 2: Your light will surely come.

(Entire cast freezes in position. A carol may be sung. Entire cast exits. Curtain.)

Questions to Think About and Discuss

1. What do you most hope for at Christmas?

2. What has you wondering this Christmas?

3. Has Christmas ever seemed ordinary to you? Explain.

4. What hope do you attach to the coming of Christ?

Witness and Servanthood

Barnabas, Where Are You?

Scene

Joan sits center stage with Characters 1, 2, and 3 seated to her right, facing her. You will need a briefcase; a large button that says, "I am capable and confident"; a book entitled How to Win at Everything; *and a large mirror inside a carrying case.*

Joan: I do appreciate your being here.

Character 1: It's the least we can do.

Character 2: We understand.

Joan: I need your support.

Character 3: We can see that. Your situation is not an easy one.

Joan: So how do I handle this. It's bigger than I am. I'm afraid.

Character 1: I'll begin. First, let me say how well you've done in articulating your challenge. It hasn't been easy for you, has it?

Joan: No. It's been a nightmare.

Character 1: I hope that you can handle what I have to say to you.

Joan: It can't be any worse than what I'm enduring now.

Character 1: Very well, Joan. Your problem is that you lack confidence.

Joan: Maybe so. I do fatigue. It's been a long struggle, and it isn't over yet.

Character 1: I brought the answer with me, Joan. I have it right here in my briefcase. *(Reaches for briefcase)*

Joan: In your briefcase?

Character 1: Right here.

(Character 1 opens briefcase and pulls out "I am capable and confident" button and hands it to Joan.)

Character 1: Here you go. Consider it a gift from a friend.

Focus

Joseph, a Levite from Cyprus, whom the apostles called Barnabas (which means Son of Encouragement), sold a field that he owned and brought the money and put it at the apostles' feet. *Acts 4:36–37 (NIV)*

Barnabas was an encourager. When the early church needed him, he was there with intentional acts of support. When St. Paul needed him, Barnabas was there, presenting Paul to the church, willing to play second fiddle and step aside when necessary. Barnabas lived up to his name. In our relationships, we all need sons and daughters of encouragement. In the drama, Joan, a contemporary Job, discovers that she needs more encouragement than her friends can offer. She needs encouragement in the Lord.

Characters

Joan (hurting, searching for help)

Characters 1, 2, and 3 (artificial, preoccupied with self, condescending)

This is what you need, Joan. Wear this, and you'll become what it says you are.

Joan: Let me get this straight. I wear this button, and my life will change? I'll be *(Looks at button)* capable and confident?

Character 1: Exactly.

Joan: If you ask me, it's like putting an ice-cream label on a can of prunes. I don't feel capable and confident, and no button is going to make me capable and confident. What makes you think it will?

Character 1: Put the button on, Joan. Trust me.

(Joan puts on button and waits with a cynical look on face.)

Joan: I feel miserable.

Character 1: Be patient.

Joan: I don't have forever, you know, to wait for some magic button to do a number on me. Life is slipping by me.

Character 2: Perhaps I should speak up here.

Joan: Please, do.

Character 2: *(Holds up book)* Here is the solution.

Joan: *(Looks skeptical)* A book?

Character 2: Not *a* book, *my* book. This is my latest book.

Joan: What's it called?

Character 2: I've called it, *How to Win at Everything.*

Joan: Quite a title.

Character 2: Read this book and you'll win, Joan! You'll win!

Joan: *(Reaches for book)* May I see it?

Character 2: *(Draws book back)* That will be $16.95. I have to make a living, you know.

Joan: I'm sorry. I don't have any money with me.

Character 2: Can you call someone for some money?

Joan: I suppose I could, but I really didn't come here to make a purchase. I came to find some encouragement. I'm lost. I'm floundering like a ship at sea. I'm not sure I can go on like this much longer.

Character 2: *(Holds up book again)* It's all right here in my book.

Joan: Can't you tell me about it? Do I have to read your book to find out?

Character 2: Some things are better said in print.

Joan: And evidently for a price too. I'll pass on the book. *(Turns to Character 3)* And that leaves you.

Character 3: No, Joanie, that leaves *you!*

Joan: *(Looks skeptical)* Okay, that leaves me.

Character 3: Correct. *(Pulls large mirror from carrying case and hands it to Joan)* Look at it, Joanie. *(Helps her hold mirror to face)* Look at that beautiful face.

Joan: Where?

Character 3: You, Joanie! You!

Joan: Please don't call me Joanie.

Character 3: You're wonderful. Look at yourself, Joanie. Dig down deep inside of that person you see—way down deep. What do you find down there, Joanie? Come on, what do you find?

Joan: Ah, depression, sadness, failure.

Character 3: Joanie! Joanie! Joanie! Look again at that image. Is that a lost and floundering loser? Is it?

Joan: It is.

Character 3: *(Looks at mirror)* Well, that's not who I see in the mirror, Joanie.

Joan: Maybe that's because you're looking at yourself in the mirror and not at me!

Character 3: Joanie ...

Joan: Joan.

Character 3: Joan, you have to pull yourself out of this thing. Reach down to find the person you want.

Joan: Right.

Character 3: You feel better now, don't you?

Joan: No, I don't.

(Joan hands mirror back to Character 3 and the button back to Character 1.)

Character 1: After all we've said?

Character 2: And the offers we've made?

Character 3: What is it you want, Joan?

Joan: I want deliverance. I want to live. I want to look at the future and smile. I want, well, I want truth and a way to find life.

Character 1: Hold on, Joan. Maybe you're asking too much of us.

Character 2: Perhaps my next book …

Character 3: Joanie, we are only people. What do you expect?

Joan: Barnabas, where are you?

Character 3: What's that?

Joan: Oh, nothing. I guess I was just looking for a little encouragement. You know, Barnabas—the New Testament figure whose name means "son of encouragement."

Character 2: I thought we were encouraging you.

Character 1: We are only people, Joan—not some biblical superstar!

Joan: I know. Maybe you've helped me after all.

Character 3: Now you're talking.

Joan: I've reached down, dug deep, and reached out, but I'm still frustrated.

Character 1: So what's left?

Joan: Maybe I need to reach up.

Character 1: Up?

Joan: I need people who point *up* to something, no, who point *to* someone who is bigger than themselves because, frankly, the three of you are not enough.

Character 2: Well, how do you like that!

Joan: Don't be offended. Barnabas is not easy to find.

Character 3: Well, we tried. We hope you find what you're looking for.

Joan: I will. I will because things are looking up. Yes, things are looking up.

(Entire cast freezes in position, then exits. Curtain.)

Questions to Think About and Discuss

1. Put into your own words Joan's discovery from her encounter with her three would-be encouragers.

2. Who in your life brings you encouragement "in the Lord"?

3. Who, right now, needs your Christ-centered encouragement?

4. Why do Christians believe that confidence and endurance are much bigger than just reaching deep inside ourselves? Why isn't that enough?

Focus

Then he said, "Jesus, remember me when You come into Your kingdom." Jesus answered him, "I tell you the truth, today you will be with Me in paradise." *Luke 23:42–43 (NIV)*

Jesus remembers us. He knows us, our needs, and our hopes. Christ hears our prayers and responds. We can trust Christ to remember us and love us, one by one.

Characters

Characters 1 and 2 (friends on a mission)

Character 3 (downcast but pliable)

What Do You Mean, You Don't Remember?

Scene

This drama is a conversation upon which the audience eavesdrops. The conversation should appear natural and unrehearsed (which means extra work at rehearsal!).

Characters 1 and 2 stand on either side of Character 3, who looks downcast. Character 1 turns to Character 2.

Character 1: Great night, isn't it?

Character 2: Beautiful! Super night. Why, I'd call it paradise!

Character 3: I've seen better.

Character 1: Well, what's got you so down?

Character 3: I don't know. Just a case of the blues, I guess.

Character 1: Aw, cheer up.

Character 3: No thanks. Maybe I'll just enjoy being miserable for a while.

Character 1: Suit yourself—just so it isn't contagious.

Character 2: I know. We'll cheer you up. Remember the time we all went bowling together, just on a lark? Now that was fun.

Character 1: *(Turns to Character 3)* Sure, and you threw the ball so hard it jumped the gutter and hit the pins on the alley next to us! Now that was funny! *(Characters 1 and 2 laugh)*

Character 3: I don't remember that. We went bowling?

Character 2: What do you mean, you don't remember?

Character 3: I don't. I remember the time you were going to pick me up for dinner and forgot about me. You left me there alone.

Character 2: Poor baby.

Character 3: I remember.

Character 1: That was more than a year ago.

Character 2: We're sorry.

Character 1: Hey, what about the time we all went Christmas caroling together. Remember how the people in the nursing home followed us around in their wheelchairs? That was great.

Character 3: Caroling? When did we go caroling?

Character 2: Give me a break.

Character 3: I don't remember caroling with you.

Character 1: What do you mean, you don't remember?

Character 3: *(Turns to Character 2)* I remember you spilling your Christmas punch on our new carpeting. Do you remember that?

Character 2: I do.

Character 3: The stain is still there. Never did come out completely.

Character 2: I feel bad.

Character 3: *(Satirically)* That's okay. We only notice it three or four times a day.

Character 1: Something tells me these blues of yours are contagious. Tell me you don't recall the good time we had over lunch last week.

Character 3: I recall lunch.

Character 1: You recall lunch! Well, that's mighty big of you. You were cutting up with the rest of us! You were laughing so loud the waiter was giving you stares!

Character 3: It doesn't seem such a big deal right now. Anyway, who got the check?

Character 1: You offered!

Character 3: Because you looked my way. You expected it, didn't you?

Character 1: My goodness, you've got the most selective memory I've ever heard!

Character 3: I guess my blues have just gotten the best of me.

Character 2: I'd say our paradise isn't what it once was.

Character 1: Funny, how one bad mood can come in like a cloud and rain gloom on everything.

Character 3: Reminds me of the big storm back in July of [fill in year] …

Character 2: Is that all you can remember—the bad news?

Character 3: And the record storm of [fill in year] …

Character 2: Can you believe this?

Character 3: The time I slipped on the driveway and cracked two ribs.

Character 1: Maybe you should go sit in a dark room for a while—alone. *(Silence)*

Character 2: So this is where we leave it, all darkness and gloom?

Character 3: I guess.

Character 1: Sure glad God's memory doesn't work like yours.

Character 3: Somehow I knew you'd bring God into this.

Character 1: God remembers what matters most—the sacrifice of His Son, our faith, and love and trust.

Character 2: And God forgets the bad things about us—our sins—like stains on the carpet.

Character 1: And that's paradise—to be remembered favorably by God.

Character 3: This isn't paradise. This is [name of state/province].

Character 1: But we all could ask God's help in bringing paradise a little closer to home, couldn't we? *(Silence)* Well?

Character 3: I suppose.

Character 2: Hey, remember the time we …

Character 3: Hey, all right, I surrender. I remember the bowling and the Christmas caroling and the lunch. I remember it all. There. Satisfied?

Character 2: So you do remember?

Character 3: Sure.

Character 2: Then why didn't you say so?

Character 3: I wasn't in the mood for paradise.

Character 2: And now?

Character 3: Let's just say I'm warming up to the idea.

Character 2: Well, what do you know—a ray of light!

Character 1: Hope springs eternal.

Character 2: We'll settle for that.

Character 3: Paradise and [name of state/province] still seem mutually exclusive to me. *(Entire cast walks to rear of stage)*

Character 2: We'll work on it. Stay warm to the idea.

Character 1: We haven't heard the last word on paradise yet.

(Entire cast exits. Curtain.)

Questions to Think About and Discuss

1. What memories cheer you up?

2. Why do we remember our sins if God chooses not to recall them?

3. What keeps you from paradise?

4. What bad memory do you need God's help to relinquish?

5. What makes you want to be in paradise?

6. How are we like the thieves that were crucified with Christ?

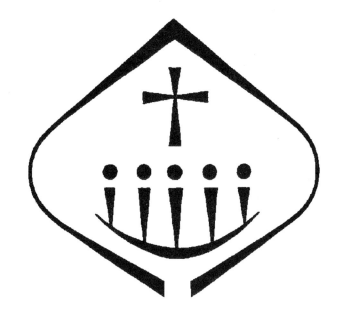

Witness and Service

Focus

Then [Jesus] called the crowd to Him along with His disciples and said: "If anyone would come after Me, he must deny himself and take up his cross and follow Me." *Mark 8:34 (NIV)*

Those who follow Christ carry a cross. To carry a cross, however, is to go against the grain of the world. With a cross comes mockery and misunderstanding. We who carry crosses endure in the promise and strength of Jesus.

Characters

Storyteller (engaging, animated)

Crossbearer (confident at first but loses confidence as drama unfolds)

Characters 1, 2, and 3 (questioning, accusatory)

The Man with the Cross

Scene

Storyteller stands at lectern or among the congregation. You will need a large wooden cross (6 to 8 feet high) for the Crossbearer to carry. Set a desk and chair stage right and another chair stage left.

Characters 1, 2, and 3 enter and take positions stage left. Crossbearer enters down center aisle, bearing cross, and walks to center stage as Storyteller reads opening lines.

Storyteller: Once there was a man who always carried a cross. Wherever he went, his cross went with him. And wherever he went, people asked him questions. Every day he was "cross examined" by someone. Some questions were whispered under the breath:

Character 1: Who does he think he is, anyway?

Storyteller: Some questions were more direct and sarcastic:

Character 2: Say, buddy, how long have you had this Messiah complex?

Storyteller: And some questions were probing and thoughtful:

Character 3: I wonder why someone would carry a cross in public like that. Does anybody know his story?

Storyteller: His story was, well, his story was the same every time they asked. He simply said,

Crossbearer: I must carry a cross, and so must you, if you want to follow Him.

Storyteller: That is what he said, "I must carry a cross, and so must you, if you want to follow Him." He was not a peculiar-looking man. In fact, he looked to those who knew him as he had always looked—well-dressed, clean-cut, that sort of thing. Only there was this big difference—the cross he carried. He didn't hesitate to take the cross to work with him.

(Crossbearer walks stage right to chair and desk. Characters 1, 2, and 3 stay stage left.)

Storyteller: As he sat at his desk in that place where money is made and deals are cut, he balanced the cross on his shoulder. The cross examination continued, this time from his co-workers.

Character 1: Has he changed? Have you noticed? He's changed, hasn't he?

Storyteller: No one could answer. He looked the same—except for that cross!

Character 2: I heard he got religion, I mean, really got it. Why do people who get some spiritual awakening always seem to go off the deep end?

Storyteller: An interesting question. Still others wondered out loud about the place of the cross in the work place:

Character 3: How does he expect to get anything done with that thing on his back?

Crossbearer: I must carry a cross, and so must you, if you want to follow Him.

Storyteller: And that is what he said. It was cumbersome, that cross. *(Crossbearer moves back to chair stage left)* Imagine fitting yourself and a cross on a commuter train going home. The questions were always there.

Character 2: *(In a child's voice)* Mommy, what's wrong with the man with the cross? Did he do something bad?

Storyteller: Children have a heart for such people.

Character 2: *(In a child's voice)* Can someone help him with the cross or does he have to carry it alone?

Storyteller: Help was not the response. Instead more questions came.

Character 3: Say, mister, do you have to make a scene? Can't you keep your religion to yourself?

Character 1: Did you ever think, buddy, what it would be like if we all carried crosses around? Think of those around you, will you?

Storyteller: But all he said was,

Crossbearer: I must carry a cross, and so must you, if you want to follow Him.

(Crossbearer walks to church pew in front of sanctuary.)

Storyteller: When Sunday came, the man with the cross

didn't hesitate to carry his cross into church and sit where he always sat. When he entered, some people stood up, thinking it was a procession of some sort. Then they realized that it was just him—and his cross. The whispers began immediately.

Character 2: Talk about up-staging the pastor!

Character 1: Why don't we all just stick with jewelry!

Character 3: What does it mean?

Storyteller: "What *does* it mean?" they asked him out in the narthex. *(Crossbearer stands and walks center stage.)* And all he could say was,

Crossbearer: I must carry a cross, and so must you, if you want to follow Him.

Storyteller: Then the man went on his way home again—carrying his cross.

(Crossbearer exits and leaves cross backstage or out of view of audience then reenters and walks center stage.)

Storyteller: And the next time he was seen, he carried no cross. People were more comfortable now. They stopped asking questions and whispering. The cross examinations stopped. Now they only said,

Character 1: Now this is better.

Character 2: Back to your senses, huh, old friend?

Character 3: We were worried about you for a moment there.

Storyteller: But some still wondered.

Character 3: What did it mean?

Storyteller: Only now the man was a man *without* a cross. And he had nothing to say. People liked it that way.

Character 1: Yes, that's better, definitely better.

Storyteller: The lesson from our story? We'll make it easy for you. Those who carry crosses find questions and troubles. It was that way with the One who carried a cross for us and put crosses on our backs; and it will be that way for us. But you can say this about crossbearers, at least they have something to say when the world asks questions—something like:

Crossbearer: *(Addresses audience)* I must carry a cross, and so must you, if you want to follow Him.

(Entire cast freezes in position, then exits. Curtain.)

Questions to Think About and Discuss

1. Which is emphasized more in the church today: the glory of following Christ or the cost of following Christ?

2. How can people carry a cross in their work place?

3. The man with the cross was misunderstood by others. What are some common misunderstandings about Christ today? about Christians?

4. What do you think caused the man with the cross to leave it behind?

5. What opportunities do you have to make genuine sacrifices for others out of gratitude for what Christ has done for you?

Focus

When Jesus landed and saw a large crowd, He had compassion on them and healed their sick. *Matthew 14:14 (NIV)*

In hard times, we need the healing touch and care of another. Jesus had compassion on those who were hurting and acted on His compassion. Healing can come about in just that simple process—compassion combined with action. This drama focuses on how easily we philosophize away our compassion and hinder our own healing actions.

Characters

Storyteller (engaging, animated)

Man (disheveled, intense, nervous, pleading)

Characters 1, 2, and 3 (philosophically bent, cold)

The Man with Cockleburs

Scene

Storyteller may stand at lectern, among the congregation, or stage left. Man stands center stage with Characters 1, 2, and 3 stage right. No set design or props are necessary.

Entire cast enters and takes positions.

Storyteller: Once there was a man with cockleburs. If you're wondering what a cocklebur is, then let us turn to Mr. Webster, who describes a cocklebur as follows: "the prickly fruit of a cocklebur that readily attaches itself to any passing object." You know cockleburs. They stick to your clothing and your socks when you take a walk in a field. They can be very irritating and even painful if not removed. Anyway, there was a man with cockleburs. He had them at his ankles.

Man: *(Bends to touch ankles)* Ouch!

Storyteller: And he had them at his neck.

Man: *(Touches neck)* O-o-o-o-oh-h-h! That hurts. *(Pantomimes sitting down)*

Storyteller: He also had them where he sat.

Man: *(Stands immediately)* Ow-w-w-e-e-e!

Storyteller: He was clearly uncomfortable. Those who knew him tried to be understanding.

Character 1: You have my sympathy, *(Man shakes and trembles.)*

Storyteller: Said one. Another said,

Character 2: You should really have those taken care of.

Storyteller: While a third dear friend said,

Character 3: You must really be uncomfortable.

Storyteller: It's a fine thing to have such understanding friends. No wonder that the man responded by saying,

Man: Can you help me?

Storyteller: He meant his friends. He wondered if they would help him.

Man: Will you help me? They are, after all, only cockleburs.

Character 1: Oh, cockleburs. You mean the prickly fruit of a cocklebur that readily attaches itself to any passing object?

Man: Exactly,

Storyteller: Said the man with hope building by the second.

Character 1: Wouldn't know where to begin,

Storyteller: Said the friend, while another said simply,

Character 2: They must have a specialist for that!

Man: A specialist? For cockleburs? Whatever happened to friends you can count on? Am I to live with my pain?

Storyteller: And as if to echo the man's own words, the friend said,

Character 3: It's only cockleburs. You said so yourself. Live with them for a while. Maybe you're meant to be uncomfortable.

Character 1: Yes, maybe God wants you to be uncomfortable.

Character 2: Maybe you've been bad, and God is punishing you.

Man: With cockleburs?

Storyteller: Protested the man, whose patience by now was running thin.

Character 3: Maybe this is your "thorn in the flesh." Yes, for sure, a thorn in the flesh! You're in good company. St. Paul had one. Sit down and bear your cross.

Man: I can't sit down! That's the point! It's very uncomfortable!

Character 1: Would you call it a sharp pain or an ache? On a pain scale of 1 to 10, 10 being the most painful, how would you rate this discomfort?

Man: What is this? A scientific exploration of cockleburs?

Storyteller: The man with the cockleburs was clearly getting angry.

Character 2: You have our pity.

Character 3: And you certainly have our understanding.

Man: Fine. Now could I have your hand to pluck out a few cockleburs from your old buddy's body?

Storyteller: The three friends huddled, caucused, and whispered. *(Characters 1, 2, and 3 huddle and whisper)* Then they spoke.

Character 1: You will need to have them removed by someone else.

Storyteller: And that was that. "You will need to have them removed by someone else."

Man: But why? Why won't you help me?

Character 2: Insurance concerns.

Character 3: They may be poisonous.

Man: Cockleburs?

Character 1: They are not all on the most accessible parts of your body.

Man: Well, pardon me. Next time I'll plan ahead and get them exactly where you like them. What else? There's more, I bet.

Character 2: We do not want to risk interfering in divine punishment or retribution.

Man: You what?

Character 3: If God gave you cockleburs, let God take them away!

Storyteller: And that was that. Somewhere in town, there may still be a fellow with cockleburs unattended. If you see him, would you help him? He can use a hand—in the right places. The moral of this parable? Those in pain may be left alone by friends who favor fear and philosophy over real compassion. It's a thorny problem, I know, this pain we bear in life. But it's no excuse for others to feel that they must bear their pain alone.

(Entire cast exits. Curtain.)

Questions to Think About and Discuss

1. Share a time when you were hurting, and it seemed as if no one cared.

2. What motivation do Christians have for actively involving themselves in the hurts of others? *(See 1 John 3:16, 4:19.)*

3. Jesus' story of the Good Samaritan includes others who could have helped the hurting man but chose not to get involved. Read Luke 10:25–37. What were their reasons for not helping?

4. Who are today's hurting people who are often neglected by those who could help?

Focus

For the Son of Man came to seek and to save what was lost. *Luke 19:10 (NIV)*

Jesus can leave us feeling safe and secure. As we follow Him, though, we may need to sacrifice our security for the sake of seeking the lost. Christ did that for us. Bearing a witness and a cross, He asks us to do the same.

Characters

Shepherd (gentle, warm, mysterious, confident)

Characters 1, 2, 3, 4, and 5 (the sheep—enthusiastic, cautious)

To Seek What Is Lost

Scene

This drama requires significant movement. If it is presented in the sanctuary, Shepherd and Sheep may move around among the congregation. The sheep costumes can be as simple as wearing a woollike hood draped over the shoulders. Shepherd dresses as either an ancient or contemporary herdsman and carries a large staff. Sheep follow in line behind him.

Shepherd enters stage right, leading Characters 1, 2, 3, 4, and 5 [referred to as Sheep in stage directions unless specific actions are required]. Sheep follow Shepherd to center stage and huddle behind him.

Character 1: We are sheep, and *(Points to Shepherd)* he is the shepherd.
All of us follow. The shepherd will lead.

Character 2: We are the sheep, and he is the shepherd.
The shepherd will give us what we need.

Character 1: It's good being a sheep.

Character 2: Very good.

Character 1: It's very good being in this flock.

Character 2: Very good.

Character 1: He is a good shepherd.

Character 2: He is a very good shepherd indeed.

Character 1: We are the sheep, and he is the shepherd.
All of us follow. The shepherd will lead.

Character 2: We are the sheep, and he is the shepherd.
The shepherd provides us with all that we need.

Character 3: *(Counts Sheep)* 1-2-3-4-5. All here. Watch him now. He's ready to turn. *(Shepherd turns toward Sheep)* He's counting. I knew he would count. He always counts.

(Shepherd turns and, with head motion, counts Sheep.)

Character 3: We're all here, sir. All present and accounted for. You can count on us.

(Shepherd raises staff and begins to walk.)

Character 3: Oops. Here goes. We're moving again.

Character 4: Do we follow?

Character 1: Do we like green grass in the summertime? Of course we follow.

(Sheep follow Shepherd, ending stage left.)

Character 4: I'm not sure I know this place.

Character 3: Trust him.

Character 5: Why should we trust him?

Character 3: Has he ever let you down? He is a popular shepherd. Ask the others.

Character 5: *(Turns to Characters 1 and 2)* Well?

Character 1: A popular shepherd.

Character 2: Oh, yes, yes, a very popular shepherd and very reliable too.

Character 1: Well put.

Character 2: Very well put, if I say so myself.

Character 3: Look around you. Are these green pastures or what!

(Shepherd raises staff.)

Character 1: There! The staff again. Let's go.

(Shepherd leads Sheep down one aisle and up another. Sheep follow, chanting.)

Character 1: Follow the leader. Follow the man.
   Follow the shepherd, staff in his hand.

Character 2: Follow the leader. Follow the man.
   Follow the herdsman as best as you can.

(As Sheep walk during Character 3's next section of dialog, Characters 4 and 5 break from flock and exit at nearest door. Characters 1, 2, and 3 continue to follow Shepherd and don't notice the exit of Characters 4 and 5. Shepherd doesn't see them leave either.)

Character 3: We are a flock, a family, a clan.
   We are all one, the sheep and the man.
   He'll take us to pastures. He'll call us by name.
   He'll give us his love, every one, just the same.

(Shepherd and remaining Sheep stop center stage. Shepherd turns to face Sheep.)

Character 3: Oh, here he goes again. Watch him. Watch him count us again.

(Character 3 looks back and notices Characters 4 and 5 are gone and looks startled. Shepherd counts using head motion.)

Character 1: Something is wrong.

Character 2: Very wrong indeed.

(Shepherd looks in every direction for missing Sheep.)

Character 3: We're not all here! That's what's wrong. The shepherd sees it. He knows.

Character 1: I am worried.

Character 2: I am very worried.

Character 3: He is a good shepherd. Remember?

Character 1: We are the sheep, and he is the shepherd. All of us follow. The shepherd will lead.

Character 2: We are the sheep, and he is the shepherd. The shepherd provides us with all that we need.

Character 3: That's right.

(Shepherd turns to Sheep.)

Shepherd: You must follow me now. We are too far from home. I cannot leave you here. Follow me. It will be dangerous. I must find the two strays. You cannot stay here. Not now. *(Raises staff)* Follow me.

(Shepherd walks, but Sheep don't follow. Shepherd stops.)

Shepherd: I know you are afraid. I will be honest with you. It is dangerous where we are going. Trust me. *(Raises staff)* Follow me.

(Shepherd holds staff high and freezes in position as Characters 1, 2, and 3 speak.)

Character 1: I am afraid.

Character 2: I am very afraid.

Character 3: I don't understand. Does he care more for those two than he does for us three? This is not like him, not like him at all. "He'll give us his love, every one, just the same." That's the way it goes.

Character 1: Where are the other two?

Character 2: They are gone.

Character 3: He wants to find them and take us with him. He's going where we haven't gone before.

(Shepherd lowers, then raises staff.)

Shepherd: I'm losing time. It's getting dark. The clouds are rolling in. I'll have to go now. *(Raises staff higher still)* Follow me!

(Shepherd walks 10 paces down center aisle, away from Sheep, and doesn't look back. Shepherd stops.)

Character 3: He isn't sure. Which will it be? The two strays or the three?

Character 1: He wants us to follow. I think we should follow.

Character 2: I am sure we should follow. Very sure.

(Character 2 starts but Character 3 stops Character 2.)

Character 3: Wait. See what he does. He will not leave us here for two runaways. And we have never been where he is going.

Character 1: But remember, he is a good shepherd.

Character 2: We are a flock, a family, a clan.
We are all one, the sheep and the man.

Character 3: We're not all one anymore. We are divided, split, and scattered. He will have to decide—the strays or us.

(Shepherd turns to face Sheep, raises staff, and speaks gently.)

Shepherd: You are my sheep, and I am your shepherd. Follow me. It may be dangerous, but I will go before you. Come.

(Shepherd waits in silence with staff raised, he hesitates, then walks alone to distant exit.)

Character 1: We must catch him before he's out of sight.

Character 2: Shepherd, I want to come, but …

Character 3: He has gone for the strays and left us behind.

Character 1: We should have followed.

Character 2: I know we should have followed. So what happens now?

Character 3: We wait. He may come back for us.

Character 1: After he finds them!

Character 2: *If* he finds them! It is dangerous where he is going.

Character 1: He may never come back.

Character 3: He has made his choice.

Character 1: And we have made ours.

(Entire cast freezes in position, then exits. Curtain.)

Questions to Think About and Discuss

1. Read Jesus' parable of the lost sheep in Luke 15:1–7. What are the similarities and differences between that parable and this drama?

2. One of the sheep in the drama says, "And we have never been where he is going." Many Christians have never followed Jesus into risky situations for the sake of Christian witness. What makes it difficult for us to follow where Jesus leads?

3. What is your church doing to reach those who do not know Christ or those who are "strays" from the family of faith?

4. In Mark 8:34, Jesus says that those who come after Him must take up a cross and follow Him. Bearing a cross for Christ means being willing to suffer for His cause. Where do you see modern Christians willingly bearing crosses for Christ?

5. Do you think the church is on earth primarily to be cared for by Christ or primarily to follow Christ into a courageous search for the lost? If your answer is both, which area should take priority?

Focus

[Jesus said,] "You will be My witnesses." *Acts 1:8 (NIV)*

Christ calls us to be His witnesses. Willing or not, He wants us and needs us to share the wonders of His love. Every Christian is personally accountable to God for the role as a witness to Christ.

Characters

Messenger (representative of Christ, dressed in white, carries own podium)

Congregation (audience or congregation)

Everyman (wears casual clothes)

The Reluctant Witness

Scene

Print this drama completely as a bulletin or program insert so that the congregation/audience can read its part. The congregation/audience part is printed in boldface. Messenger can be dressed in white. Everyman, as in medieval morality plays, represents all of us, but here, Everyman speaks for all Christians who have ever wondered about their role as witnesses of Christ. Messenger stands center stage on podium or soap box. Everyman faces Messenger, standing between audience and Messenger.

Messenger enters, sets podium center stage, and stands on it. Everyman enters and faces Messenger.

Messenger: You will be my witnesses!

Congregation: Yes, Lord, we will.

Messenger: *(Looks at Everyman)* And you will be my witness!

Everyman: Sure, Lord, *(Points to congregation)* I'm with them.

Messenger: No, not by association or osmosis. *You* will be my witness.

Everyman: But you don't understand. I …

Messenger: You will be my witness.

Everyman: Who are you anyway?

Messenger: I am here to speak for the Lord.

Everyman: Well, whoever you are, as I said, I'm with them.

Messenger: Not good enough. The Lord needs you.

Everyman: We have a fine pastor. He speaks for all of us.

Messenger: One witness per church is not enough.

Everyman: I am not a good talker.

Messenger: The Lord has heard you talk about football, politics, the latest movie, and the economy. You seem to talk quite well.

Everyman: That's different.

Congregation: We have heard our friend here talk. He's a good talker indeed.

Everyman: *(Turns to congregation)* You're not helping.

Messenger: There is more to being a witness than talking.

Everyman: I'm listening.

Messenger: The way you are, what you do, the integrity of your life—these are all a part of your witness.

Everyman: Let me think about it.

Messenger: Think about what?

Everyman: About being a witness.

Congregation: Yes, that's a good idea. Our friend here will think about being a witness.

Messenger: There is no need to think about it. You are.

Everyman: What do you mean, I am?

Messenger: You are a witness for the Lord, every minute, every day. Even when you're not aware of it, even when you'd rather not hear about it, you're a witness to the Lord's power and love.

Everyman: I am?

Messenger: You are. You're a Christian, aren't you?

Everyman: I am.

Congregation: We all are!

Messenger: Then you are all witnesses, just as Christ said, to everyone who hears you and watches you live. And that leaves only one question.

Everyman: What's that?

Messenger: What kind of a witness are you?

(Entire cast freezes in position, then exits. Curtain.)

Questions to Think About and Discuss

1. Many of God's greatest spokespersons have at first been reluctant witnesses. What excuses did Moses give when called to speak for God? *(See Exodus 4:10.)* Isaiah? *(See Isaiah 6:5.)* Jeremiah? *(See Jeremiah 1:6.)* What excuses do we give when God calls us to speak?

2. What kinds of Christian witness are highlighted in the drama?

3. Why do you think we can talk so well about some things and seem so tongue-tied when it comes to sharing our faith?

4. Right now, who is listening and watching as you present your role as a Christian witness? That is, to whom are you witnessing today?

The Story of Jonah

Scene

This drama is most suitable for a Rally Day service, for presentation in a camp setting, as a school chapel, part of a youth event, or as a Sunday school opening. Jonah should wear a robe and hard hat. Captain and Sailors need sailor's hats. To portray the Fish, you'll need a sheet or tarp large enough to be held over the heads of eight people. You'll also need a crown for the King of Nineveh and camouflage clothing for the Plant.

No rehearsal (or a very brief one) is necessary if you decide to choose players from the audience. Instruct them to pantomime actions to match your words. You might need to add some of the stage directions into your dramatic reading if you are using an unrehearsed cast. Storyteller needs to be flexible and fun-loving to move the cast through the story.

The audience or congregation takes an active role in the drama. Signs with large numbers or finger signals from Storyteller will cue a certain group in the audience to shout their line. Before the performance, divide the audience into five sections. Rehearse each section so they recognize their cue and know their line. The group numbers in boldface in the script indicate audience participation. The following lines are for the five groups.

> ***Group 1:*** *Oh, Nineveh, you are so-o-o-o bad!*
>
> ***Group 2:*** *Say, Jonah, you're not doin' well at all!*
>
> ***Group 3:*** *Makes storm sounds such as the wind whistling and the waves crashing.*
>
> ***Group 4:*** *Cheers and applauds.*
>
> ***Group 5:*** *Laughs.*

Storyteller stands at lectern to read script. Jonah stands center stage.

Once there was a man named Jonah, an ordinary man, not rich, not poor. One thing about Jonah, though, he loved to argue. He could be hardheaded *(Jonah taps hard hat)* and stubborn. He could even look mean sometimes. *(Jonah looks mean)*

Focus

But Jonah ran away from the LORD. *Jonah 1:3 (NIV)*

Jonah's story is a story of God getting done what is necessary, despite Jonah's excuses, complaints, and escapes. To see Jonah is to see ourselves—struggling with God's will, going our own way, and still being taught and loved by God.

Characters

Storyteller (the only speaking part)

Jonah

Captain

Two Sailors

Fish (eight people holding tarp or sheet over their heads)

King of Nineveh

Plant

Worm

Even when Jonah received a message from God, he argued. One time God told Jonah that He had an errand for him. *(Jonah puts hand to ear)* God said, "Jonah, I have an errand for you. Go to Nineveh **(Group 1)** and tell that town they'd better repent of their sins before I turn them into a smoldering heap of ash. I'll give them 40 days. Then watch out!"

(Jonah puts index finger to temple) Jonah thought for a moment and then said, "God, … forget it." Instead of heading for Nineveh, Jonah caught a ship for Tarshish, which was just the opposite direction. **(Group 2)** As the ship set sail, Jonah sacked out. *(Jonah lies down on floor. Captain and Sailors enter and stand in line, swaying as if on board ship.)*

Now God didn't like this at all. So He caused a storm to come up, *(Captain and Sailors rock more rapidly)* scaring the bejiggers out of the ship's crew. *(Captain and Sailors stop rocking, raise hands, and look scared)* The winds blew **(Group 3)** and blew **(Group 3)** and blew **(Group 3)**.

Then the captain woke up Jonah. *(Captain walks to Jonah and shakes him awake. Jonah stands and rubs eyes.)* Jonah asked the brilliant question, "Are we almost there?" **(Group 2)**

"There?" said the captain. *(Points up)* "Look at those winds!" **(Group 3)** The winds blew. **(Group 3)** The sailors shivered in fright. *(Sailors shiver)* Jonah admitted, "Guys, it's probably all my fault. God is after me because I've done something wrong." **(Group 2)**

The captain said, "Well, pray, dimwit."

Jonah said, "It's too late for that. Throw me overboard."

"I could never do that," said the captain. The winds blew! **(Group 3)** People got angry at Jonah. **(Group 2)** Finally, they dumped him into the sea. *(Sailors pantomime throwing Jonah out of the boat.)*

Immediately the winds stopped. **(Group 4)** As Jonah floated away from the ship, he could hear the captain *(Captain falls to knees)* speaking prayers to God. *(Captain and Sailors exit.)*

Soon enough, Jonah found himself floating toward what looked to be a giant cave. *(Fish enters up center aisle toward Jonah)* But as he got closer, Jonah noticed the cave had eyes over its mouth. **(Group 2)** Suddenly Jonah found himself being swallowed whole by a gigantic fish. *(Fish "swallows" Jonah by wrapping him under the sheet/tarp. Fish "swims" down center aisle with Jonah inside.)* And there inside that big fish's belly, Jonah sat and sat.

There in the gut of that giant fish, Jonah got religious again. **(Group 4)** He asked God to forgive him and to give him another chance to obey. He even promised to go Nineveh. **(Group 1)**

Then something phenomenal happened. The fish, who had fulfilled its God-ordained purpose and whose digestive system was probably quite disturbed, upchucked Jonah right on dry ground. The fish gagged and gagged until finally it threw Jonah up on land. *(Fish opens up sheet/tarp and shoves Jonah back toward center stage)* **(Group 4)** You might say Jonah owed his whole life to a gut reaction. **(Group 5)** *(Fish exits.)*

Jonah wept tears of joy once he got over the shock of being regurgitated. And sure enough, he went to the city of Nineveh. **(Group 4)**

The people of Nineveh were just as Jonah had expected—rude, crude, and mean. **(Group 1)** When Jonah told *(Pantomimes preaching)* them they had better repent or in 40 days they'd be no more, the people of Nineveh laughed and laughed. **(Group 5)** *(King of Nineveh enters and pantomimes declaration.)* But the king of Nineveh got a little worried and declared, "Shush, you crazy people!" And Jonah told his story, and the whole city turned around. It was an amazing thing. Everybody actually repented of their sins! **(Group 4)** *(King of Nineveh exits.)*

And God saved the people of Nineveh from being smoked on the spot. Everybody was happy. **(Group 5)** I mean, everybody except one person. Guess who? Right. Jonah. He was back to his old nasty, argumentative self. **(Group 2)**

Jonah said to God, *(Looks up and points finger)* "You're too soft for me, Lord. I knew You'd do this. You should have nuked the whole territory. Instead, You show them mercy! I'm depressed. *(Looks depressed)* If you don't mind, I'll just lapse into severe depression, loneliness, anger, and despondency." *(Jonah sits on stage, despondent.)*

God said gently, "Jonah, do you really think you have a right to be angry?" Jonah didn't answer. **(Group 2)**

Now with Jonah out somewhere near the boondocks, God caused a castor oil plant to grow up over Jonah. *(Plant enters and "grows up" over Jonah)* Jonah, it turns out, became a real plant-lover. He loved that castor oil plant because it gave him pleasant shade in the hot afternoons that were characteristic of that region somewhere near the boondocks. Jonah was very happy. *(Jonah raises head and smiles)* That whole day, he enjoyed the shade of his new friend.

(Worm slinks across floor toward Plant) But the next morning, God made a little worm attack that plant and kill it. *(Worm attacks Plant, which falls to the ground. Worm slithers away.)* Jonah was very upset. He told God that he'd just as soon die. He didn't have a friend left. Even his tall green friend was dead. **(Group 2)**

Then God said, *(Jonah begins with head down, then raises it to listen with hand to ear)* "Jonah, you feel sorry for that little plant that you had for only one day. What about Me? I created all those people in Nineveh. I love them. Don't I have a right to save them if I choose?"

And, as the Bible tells it, Jonah was finally getting the message—God can do what He wants to do, and He'll get it done even if we get in His way. God can be very creative when it comes to getting His mission done. Ask Jonah. He knows. **(Group 4)**

(Jonah makes okay sign, then exits. Curtain.)

Questions to Think About and Discuss

1. What assignments or commands from God are difficult for you to obey?

2. Why do you think Jonah did not want to go to Nineveh?

3. Whom is it hard for you to love? Who makes Christian love a real challenge for you because of the way he or she is?

4. Did God surprise you in this story? What surprised you most?

5. What do you learn about God from this story?

6. What do you learn about being a witness for Christ?

124

Focus

I will not leave you as orphans; I will come to you.
John 14:18 (NIV)

From the very beginning, God saw that it was not good for us to be alone. Christ promised that we would not be left behind as orphans. That promise contains a challenge to the church to be the heart and hands of Christ reaching out to the lonely.

Characters

Characters 1 and 2 (detached, philosophical, cautious)

Character 3 (curious, cautious)

It Isn't Easy Being Alone

Scene

Be sure to accent the separation between Character 3 (the lonely individual) and Characters 1 and 2 (the church) by placing them clearly at a distance from each other.

Characters 1 and 2 stand stage right. Character 3 stands stage left.

Character 1: *(Points to Character 3)* There she is, alone again.

Character 2: She's almost always alone.

Character 1: I suppose she likes it that way.

Character 2: Why don't you ask her?

Character 1: Well, because she probably wants to be left alone. *(Silence)* Maybe she thinks she's better than everybody else.

Character 2: Maybe she thinks she's worse than everybody else. *(Character 3 looks across at Characters 1 and 2.)*

Character 1: Sh-h-h. I think she's listening. *(Silence. Character 3 looks down.)* Maybe we should invite her over.

Character 2: Over?

Character 1: Over here to join us.

Character 2: Why would she want to do that?

Character 1: I don't know. It isn't easy being alone, you know. *(Turns to Character 3)* Excuse me.

Character 2: What are you doing?

Character 1: I'm talking to her. Is that a problem?

Character 2: Suit yourself.

Character 1: *(Turns to Character 3)* Excuse me?

(Character 3 looks at Character 1, then looks down.)

Character 1: I said, "Excuse me!"

Character 3: *(Looks at Character 1 again)* Yes?

Character 1: We see you are alone.

Character 3: Yes, I am.

Character 1: Have you been alone long?

Character 3: Quite a long time.

Character 1: It must be hard.

Character 3: It isn't easy being alone.

Character 1: *(Turns to Character 2)* I told you. *(Turns to Character 3)* You're welcome to come over here and join us.

Character 2: Yes, come on over.

Character 3: Why should I?

Character 1: So you're not alone.

Character 2: So you're with somebody.

Character 3: Why don't you come over here? Why don't you come join me?

Character 2: Now that's a presumptuous thing to say! Imagine that! She wants us to join her over there!

Character 1: I told you. She thinks she's better than everybody else.

Character 3: I do not. It isn't easy being alone.

Character 1: Then shake off your pride and come on over. We're nice.

Character 2: You'll like us.

Character 3: It will make you feel good if I come over, won't it?

Character 1: Sure.

Character 2: I suppose. *(Points to audience)* After all, they're watching. It'll look good. It shows our, ah, our openness, our inclusiveness. In one move on your part, we'll increase our membership by 50 percent—a splendid growth rate.

Character 1: These are important realities for the church as we enter a new century.

Character 3: So you are the church?

Character 2: We are—one small segment.

Character 1: "Wherever two or three are gathered," you know.

Character 3: Why won't you gather over here?

Character 2: You come to us. It's better.

Character 3: I thought Jesus talked about seeking the one lost sheep.

Character 1: It's easier if the sheep finds her own way home. It's up to *ewe*. Get it? It's up to *ewe*, E-W-E. That's a female sheep.

Character 3: Very humorous.

Character 1: You're not coming over, are you?

Character 3: I'll have to think about it. Somehow I feel more like a statistic than a lost sheep. I wish you'd see that *you* entering my aloneness is very important to me.

Character 2: We invited you. What more do you want?

Character 3: I think you call it ministry.

Character 1: Aw, come on, a few steps and you're back in the fold.

Character 3: It isn't easy being alone. It isn't easy stepping into a fellowship either—joining, belonging—when you've been alone as long as I have. These things are difficult.

Character 2: What if we meet you halfway?

Character 3: I feel like I'm buying a used car.

Character 1: Come on over. Will you ple-e-e-ase come on over?

Character 2: Don't beg. She'll make the move. She has to, doesn't she?

Character 1: Sure.

Character 2: *(Turns to audience)* It is presumptuous, wouldn't you say, that she expects us to come and, well, rescue her from her loneliness? Well, isn't it? *(Silence)*

Character 1: I'm telling you, she likes being alone.

Character 2: We gave it our best shot.

Character 1: What more can anyone ask?

Character 2: Let's go. *(Exits stage right)*

Character 1: Okay. *(Exits but first walks toward Character 3)* Last chance. We're on our way ...

Character 2: And we may not pass this way again.

Character 1: We're going ...

Character 2: Going ...

Character 1: Gone.

Character 3: And I am left alone.

(Curtain.)

Questions to Think About and Discuss

1. Does our church wait for the lost to come to us or do we take the initiative?

2. What are some not-so-healthy attitudes we may have toward those outside the church?

3. What can we do to close the distance between us and the lonely members of our community?

4. How much do we do (or not do) because people are watching us?

5. When have you felt like an orphan?

6. Do you think it is presumptuous of people to expect the church to care?

7. If we got serious about being Christ's heart and hands in our community, where might people find us at work?

Appendix A

Index of Dramas Appropriate for Specific Seasons or Special Days